Table of Contents

Table of Contents

GRADE 7

McGraw-Hill's
Math

New York   Chicago   San Francisco   Lisbon   London   Madrid   Mexico City
Milan   New Delhi   San Juan   Seoul   Singapore   Sydney   Toronto

The **McGraw·Hill** *Companies*

Copyright © 2011 by the McGraw-Hill Companies, Inc. All rights reserved. Printed in the United States of America. Except as permitted under the United States Copyright Act of 1976, no part of this publication may be reproduced or distributed in any form or by any means, or stored in a database or retrieval system, without the prior written permission of the publisher.

3 4 5 6 7 8 9 10 11 12 13 14 15 DOW/DOW 1 9 8 7 6 5 4 3 2

ISBN   978-0-07-174863-6
MHID   0-07-174863-6

Editorial Services: SkyBridge Publishing
Production Services: Watch This Space, Inc.
Design Services: PlanetGraham Design

Printed and bound by RR Donnelley

Cataloging-in-Publication data for this title are on file at the Library of Congress.

McGraw-Hill books are available at special quantity discounts for use as premiums and sales promotions, or for use in corporate training programs. To contact a representative please e-mail us at bulksales@mcgraw-hill.com.

This book is printed on acid-free paper.

This book is designed to help you succeed in your seventh grade mathematics study. Short lessons explain key points, while exercises help you practice what you learned.

First, begin with the **Pretest**. This will identify areas that you need additional help with, as well as areas in which you are more comfortable.

Second, read the **Table of Contents**. Seeing how a book is organized will help guide your work.

Third, look at the **10-Week Summer Study Plan**. This will help you plan your time spent in practicing the skills you will master in this book. Remember, the Summer Study Plan is only a guide for you. You may proceed more quickly on some lessons, and you may need to spend more time on other lessons.

Fourth, notice the hints included in some of the lessons following the special **Remember** feature. These will help you remember key points that often make your mathematics work easier.

Fifth, take the **Posttest**. This test will demonstrate what you mastered as well as areas you may have to return to.

Finally, remember the old saying, "Practice makes perfect." In mathematics, practice may not guarantee perfection, but it certainly makes learning easier.

10-Week Summer Study Plan

Many students will use this book as a summer study program. If that's what you are doing, here is a handy 10-week study plan that can help you make the best use of your time.

When you complete each day's assignment, check it off by marking the box. Each assignment should take you approximately 30 minutes.

	Day	Lesson(s)	Test	✔
Week 1	Monday	1.1, 1.2	Pretest	
	Tuesday	1.3		
	Wednesday	2.1, 2.2		
	Thursday	3.1		
	Friday	3.2	Lessons 1–3 Unit Test	
Week 2	Monday	4.1, 4.2, 4.3		
	Tuesday	4.4, 4.5, 4.6		
	Wednesday	4.7, 4.8		
	Thursday	5.1, 5.2		
	Friday	5.3		
Week 3	Monday	6.1, 6.2		
	Tuesday	6.3, 6.4		
	Wednesday	7.1		
	Thursday	7.2		
	Friday	7.3	Lessons 4–7 Unit Test	
Week 4	Monday	8.1, 8.2		
	Tuesday	8.3, 8.4		
	Wednesday	9.1, 9.2		
	Thursday	9.3, 9.4		
	Friday	10.1, 10.2, 10.3		
Week 5	Monday	11.1, 11.2		
	Tuesday	11.3, 11.4, 11.5		
	Wednesday	12.1, 12.2		
	Thursday	12.3, 12.4		
	Friday	12.5, 12.6	Lessons 8–12 Unit Test	

	Day	Lesson(s)	Test	✔
Week 6	Monday	13.1, 13.2		
	Tuesday	13.3, 13.4		
	Wednesday	14.1, 14.2		
	Thursday	14.3, 14.4		
	Friday	14.5, 14.6	Lessons 13–14 Unit Test	
Week 7	Monday	15.1, 15.2		
	Tuesday	16.1, 16.2		
	Wednesday	16.3, 16.4		
	Thursday	17.1, 17.2		
	Friday	17.3		
Week 8	Monday	18.1, 18.2		
	Tuesday	18.3, 18.4	Lessons 15–18 Unit Test	
	Wednesday	19.1, 19.2		
	Thursday	19.3, 19.4		
	Friday	19.5		
Week 9	Monday	19.6		
	Tuesday	19.7, 20.1		
	Wednesday	20.2, 20.3		
	Thursday	20.4, 20.5		
	Friday	21.1, 21.2	Lessons 19–21 Unit Test	
Week 10	Monday	22.1, 22.2		
	Tuesday	23.1, 23.2		
	Wednesday	24.1, 24.2		
	Thursday	24.3, 24.4		
	Friday	24.5, 24.6	Lessons 22–24 Unit Test & Posttest	

Pretest

Complete the following test items on pages 4–7.

1 Restate the number 4,587,902.453.

Expanded form: _____

Written form: _____

2 Cheryl's Department Store is having a sale. They have 145 coats in stock and are adding 55 more. If at the end of the sale they still have 25 coats in stock, how many coats did they sell? _____

3 Tracey pedals 16 miles a day on a stationary bicycle. How many miles does she pedal in the month of March? (Remember, March has 31 days.) _____

How many yards does she pedal? _____

Calculate.

4 $\begin{array}{r} 36 \\ \times\ 22 \\ \hline \end{array}$

5 $\begin{array}{r} 11 \\ \times\ 59 \\ \hline \end{array}$

6 $\begin{array}{r} 74 \\ \times\ 38 \\ \hline \end{array}$

7 $\begin{array}{r} 27 \\ \times\ 71 \\ \hline \end{array}$

8 $12\overline{)996}$

9 $38\overline{)798}$

10 $17\overline{)1821}$

11 $25\overline{)155}$

12 Bailey bought $11\frac{1}{4}$ kilograms of bird feed. On the way home, he spilled $3\frac{5}{8}$ kilograms. How much bird feed does he still have left? _____

13 Margaret mixes 1,400 centiliters of grape juice with $5\frac{2}{3}$ liters of seltzer and $\frac{2}{5}$ liters of orange juice. How many liters of punch will this make? _____

14 $1\frac{4}{15} + 7\frac{2}{5} + \frac{1}{3} =$ _____

15 $-9 + 10 - (-8) + 6(-2) + \frac{6}{-2} =$ _____

16 Solve for x: $x - 9 = 18$ _____

17 Solve for x: $2x + 5 = 15$ _____

18 What property is represented by the following equation?
$4(5 + 6) = 4 \times 5 + 4 \times 6$

_____

19 What property is represented by the following equation?
$(3 + 6) + 6 = 3 + (6 + 6)$

_____

20 $9 + (2 + 3)^2 - (6 \div 3) + 4(8 \times 3) + 4(5 - 3) =$ _____

21 Give the coordinates for the points.

A _____

B _____

C _____

D _____

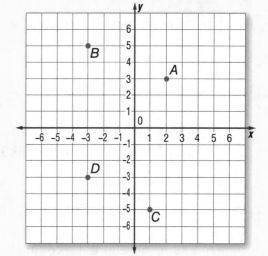

22 Restate in exponent form, then solve:

$4 \times 4 \times 4 + 2 \times 2 =$

_____

23 What is the area of the rectangle?

_____

What is the perimeter of the rectangle?

_____

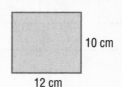

10 cm

12 cm

24 What is the area of the circle? (Use 3.14 for π.)

_____

What is the circumference of the circle?

_____

B | 5 cm | C

25 Identify the following angles as obtuse, acute, or right.

120°

90°

40°

_____   _____   _____

26 Identify the triangles as scalene, isosceles, or equilateral.

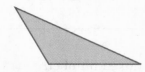

_____   _____   _____

27 Ramon spends $28.94 a month having pictures developed. He is working on a project that will take 19 months to finish. How much should he plan to spend on developing pictures for the project? _____

28 Restate 3.6 as an improper fraction and a mixed number. _____

29 Restate $4\frac{5}{8}$ as a decimal. _____

30 Is the following true or false? $\frac{5}{16} = \frac{60}{192}$ _____

31 Put the following numbers in order from least to greatest.
2.131, 2.013, 2.202, 3.003, 2.902, 1.996, 1.9, 2.009

_____

32 Drayson deposits $125 in a bank account that earns 4% simple interest. How much money will he have in the account after

1 year? _____

After 2 years? _____

33 What is the mode of the data distribution?

_____

What is the median?

_____

Stems	Leaves
1	3 5
2	3 6 9
3	3 8 8 8
4	4 4 5 6 6
5	3 4 6

34 $\frac{4}{7} \times 5\frac{4}{9} =$ _____

35 What is $\frac{3}{8}$ of 88%? _____

36 What is 30% of .675? _____

37 $.15\overline{).235}$

38 $\frac{4}{3} + \frac{2}{3} + \frac{5}{3} - \frac{1}{3} - \frac{7}{3} =$ _____

39 Identify each quadrilateral as a square, rectangle, kite, rhombus, or trapezoid.

_____ _____ _____ _____ _____

40 Identify the following figures.

_____ _____ _____

41 Restate $5\frac{6}{13}$ as an improper fraction.

_____

42 Restate $\frac{43}{16}$ as a mixed number.

_____

43 What are the chances of choosing a black marker out of a bag containing 3 red markers, 5 blue markers, 3 yellow markers, and 4 black markers?

_____

44 According to the graph, how many videos did Jamie watch in July?

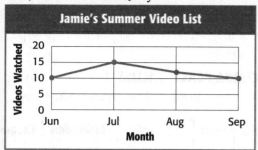

45 During which week did Kelly and Heather swim the same distance?

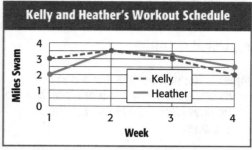

46 What fruit is most preferred by the students?

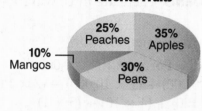

47 Peggy's score was about 30 pins higher than whose score?

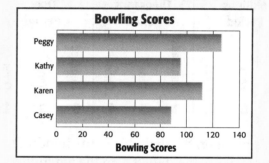

48 What is the range of the data in the box-and-whisker plot below?

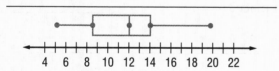

49 How much plastic wrap would you need to cover this rectangular solid?

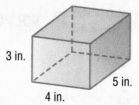

3 in.
5 in.
4 in.

50 Name two line segments. _____

Name 4 rays. _____

Name a line. _____

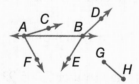

51 Fill in a Venn Diagram that displays the following data: There are two groups of students, 30 who take the bus to school and 25 who have a younger sibling in the school. There are 10 students who take the bus and who also have a younger sibling in the school.

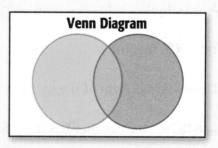

1.1

Name _____

Place Value

Place value tells you what each digit in a number means. The value of the digit depends on the place it occupies.

Example: In the number 375, the 3 is in the hundreds place, the 7 is in the tens place, and the 5 is in the ones place. So 375 means 3 hundreds + 7 tens + 5 ones.

USE A PLACE-VALUE CHART This place-value chart shows the places occupied by all the digits in the number 784,234,941.

Millions Period			Thousands Period			Ones Period		
Hundreds	Tens	Ones	Hundreds	Tens	Ones	Hundreds	Tens	Ones
7	8	4,	2	3	4,	9	4	1

In this number, the digit 7 is in the hundred millions place, the digit 8 is in the ten millions place, and so on. Places are organized into periods, or groups of three. A long string of digits is hard to read, so periods are separated by commas.

DECIMAL PLACE VALUES Decimals have place values too. Look at this place-value chart.

Tens	Ones		Tenths	Hundredths	Thousandths
2	9	.	6	2	3

The number in the chart is 29.623. Read it like this: twenty-nine and six hundred twenty-three thousandths.

NUMBER FORMS There are three ways to write numbers:

- **Standard Form:** 8,297,345
- **Expanded Form:** $(8 \times 1,000,000) + (2 \times 100,000) + (9 \times 10,000) + (7 \times 1,000) + (3 \times 100) + (4 \times 10) + (5 \times 1)$
- **Word Form:** eight million, two hundred ninety-seven thousand, three hundred forty-five.

Exercises **SOLVE**

1 In 231,739,465, the underlined digit is in which place? _Hundreds Thousands_

2 In 92.609, the number 6 is in which place? _Tenths_

3 In 2,867,403, the underlined digit is in which place? _Ones Thousands_

4 In 1.609, the number 1 is in which place? _Ones_

5 The standard form of the number 7,305.92 has the number 3 in which place? _Hundreds_

6 Which digit is in the hundredths place in the number 4,007.951? _Zero_

7 In 58,601, the underlined digit is in which place? _Tens_

8 The standard form of the number 987 has the number 7 in which place? _Ones_

9 In 842.793, the number 9 is in which place? _Hundredths_

10 In 753,964,933.41, the number 1 is in which place? __Hundredths__

11 Write the number 7,642 in expanded form. $(7 \times 1000) + (6 \times 00) + (4 \times 0) + (2 \times 1)$

12 Write the number 4,340,200 in word form. __Four million Three hundred forty thousands two hundred__

13 Write the number $(3 \times 100,000) + (2 \times 10,000) + (6 \times 1,000) + (5 \times 100) + (2 \times 10) + (3 \times 1)$ in standard form. __326521__

14 Write the number 4 million, thirty-five in standard form. __4,000,035__

15 Write the number 435,401 in expanded form. $(4 \times 100000) + (3 \times 10000) + (5 \times 1000) + (4 \times 100) + (1 \times 1)$

16 Write the number $(7 \times 10,000) + (9 \times 1,000) + (3 \times 100) + (2 \times 1)$ in word form. __7,932__

17 Write the number 7,000,213,034 in expanded form. $(7 \times 1000,000,000) + (2 \times 100000) + (1 \times 10000) + (3 \times 1000) + (4 \times 1)$

18 Write the number $(6 \times 100,000) + (8 \times 10,000) + (2 \times 1,000) + (6 \times 100) + (6 \times 10) + (5 \times 1)$ in standard form. __682665__

19 Write the number three million, four hundred thirty-one thousand, four hundred in standard form. __3,431,400__

20 Write the number 6,000,101 in expanded form. $(6 \times 1000000) + (1 \times 100) + (1 \times 1)$

1.2

Adding and Subtracting Whole Numbers

A **whole number** is a number that does not include decimals or fractions. Most people use *only* whole numbers when they count: 1, 2, 3 . . . up to as high as they need to go.

Example: Adding Whole Numbers

To add 372 + 49 + 2,891, start by lining up the **addends**, the numbers you have to add, by place value. Add each place value, *starting in the ones place.* If the total for that place value has 2 digits, write the second digit and **carry** the first digit to the next column.

$$\begin{array}{r} {\scriptstyle 1\;2\;1} \\ 372 \\ 49 \\ + \; 2891 \\ \hline 3312 \end{array}$$

Example: Subtracting Whole Numbers

To subtract 723 – 514, start by lining up the numbers by place value. Subtract each place value number, *starting in the ones place.* How do you subtract 4 ones from 3 ones? You have to **regroup**. Borrow one ten from the tens place to make the 3 ones into 13 ones.

$$\begin{array}{r} {\scriptstyle 1\,1\,3} \\ 72\cancel{3} \\ - \; 514 \\ \hline 209 \end{array}$$

Remember...

When you add or subtract whole numbers, line up the numbers by place value. Then treat *each* place value as its own problem.

Exercises   **ADD OR SUBTRACT**

1
$$\begin{array}{r} 7 \\ + \; 5 \\ \hline 12 \end{array}$$

2
$$\begin{array}{r} 33 \\ + \; 77 \\ \hline 110 \end{array}$$

3
$$\begin{array}{r} 21 \\ + \; 2100 \\ \hline 2121 \end{array}$$

4
$$\begin{array}{r} 100 \\ - \; 22 \\ \hline 78 \end{array}$$

5
$$\begin{array}{r} 1100 \\ 111 \\ + \; 11 \\ \hline 2222 \end{array}$$

6
$$\begin{array}{r} 155 \\ - \; 56 \\ \hline 99 \end{array}$$

7
$$\begin{array}{r} 122 \\ 35 \\ + \; 10 \\ \hline 167 \end{array}$$

8
$$\begin{array}{r} 45 \\ 450 \\ + \; 55 \\ \hline 550 \end{array}$$

9
$$\begin{array}{r} 237 \\ - \; 213 \\ \hline 024 \end{array}$$

10
$$\begin{array}{r} 1209 \\ - \; 311 \\ \hline 898 \end{array}$$

11
$$\begin{array}{r} 167 \\ - \; 78 \\ \hline 89 \end{array}$$

12
$$\begin{array}{r} 3456 \\ - \; 2764 \\ \hline 0692 \end{array}$$

13 1000000
      −   2345
      997655

14   211
      − 113
        98

15 5151
      + 527
      5678

16 8932
      + 378
      9310

17   33
        333
          3
      + 13
        382

18   595
          25
      + 335
        955

19   511
        1361
      − 444
        917

20   415
        3001
      ·+ 233
        3649

21 4442
      − 3333
        1109

22   34
        344
      + 43
        421

23 2001
      − 999
        1002

24   44
        555
      + 11
        610

25   48
          49
      + 761
        898

26 1811
      − 1729
        0082

27   10
          11
          12
          13
          15
      + 111
        172

28   229
      − 49
        180

29 5888
      − 790
        5098

30   544
        322
      + 1023
        1889

31 10000
      − 8888
        1112

32 1010
          11
      + 311
        1332

33   212
        355
      + 22
        589

34 1001
      − 988
        013

35   5
        1055
      + 454
        1514

36 7443
      − 4567
        2876

Name _____

Estimating Sums and Differences

What if you need only a *fairly good idea* of what a sum or a difference is? Do you still need to go through the whole process of adding or subtracting? No, you can estimate. To do that, start by **rounding** each number. Rounding changes one number into another close number that you can work with more easily.

After you decide on the digit to use for the rounding place, change *all* other digits in the number to 0. Repeat this process for all the numbers in the problem.

Your answer will *not* be exact, but it will be much better than a guess!

Example: Look at the highest place value. This is called the **rounding place**. Then look at the second highest place value. If the digit there is *less than 5*, keep the original digit in the rounding place. If the digit there is *5 or greater*, add 1 to the digit in the rounding place.

rounding place	second highest place value		rounding place	second highest place value
3611	4000		708	700
+ 5299	+ 5000		− 593	− 600
	9000			100

Exercises   ESTIMATE

1 122 + 82

2 249 + 357

3 25 + 78

4 239 + 555

5 31 + 131

6 45 + 21

7 147 + 97

8 333 − 253

9 2119 − 932

10 575 + 639

11 711 − 236

12 23 + 11

13 57450 − 4997

14 4723 + 154

15 45 + 557 + 78

16 345 + 167

17 105555 − 15559

18 3454 + 549 + 777

19 10329 − 5784

Multiplying Whole Numbers

Is multiplying more difficult than adding or subtracting? Not really—if you remember to line up the numbers by place value. Then multiply the *entire* top number by the ones place of the bottom number, and then by its tens place, and finally by its hundreds place. Think of it as doing a few single, simple problems one after the other. The answer to the entire multiplication problem is the **product**.

Example:

$$\begin{array}{r} 356 \\ \times\ 294 \\ \hline 1424 \\ (+)\ 32040 \\ (+)\ 71200 \\ \hline 104664 \end{array}$$

← placeholders

Remember...

Always use placeholder zeros in your multiplication exercises.

Exercises MULTIPLY

1 $\begin{array}{r} 5 \\ \times\ 12 \\ \hline 60 \end{array}$

2 $\begin{array}{r} 32 \\ \times\ 11 \\ \hline 352 \end{array}$

3 $\begin{array}{r} 7 \\ \times\ 19 \\ \hline 133 \end{array}$

4 $\begin{array}{r} 44 \\ \times\ 13 \\ \hline 573 \end{array}$

5 $\begin{array}{r} 41 \\ \times\ 21 \\ \hline 861 \end{array}$

6 $\begin{array}{r} 55 \\ \times\ 52 \\ \hline 2860 \end{array}$

7 $\begin{array}{r} 3 \\ \times\ 547 \\ \hline 1641 \end{array}$

8 $\begin{array}{r} 444 \\ \times\ 92 \\ \hline 64848 \end{array}$

9 $\begin{array}{r} 72 \\ \times\ 33 \\ \hline 2370 \end{array}$

10 $\begin{array}{r} 1414 \\ \times\ 63 \\ \hline 87682 \end{array}$

11 $\begin{array}{r} 59 \\ \times\ 61 \\ \hline 3179 \end{array}$

12 $\begin{array}{r} 57 \\ \times\ 19 \\ \hline 1254 \end{array}$

13 $\begin{array}{r} 68 \\ \times\ 9 \\ \hline 624 \end{array}$

14 $\begin{array}{r} 593 \\ \times\ 272 \\ \hline 125786 \end{array}$

15 $\begin{array}{r} 38 \\ \times\ 99 \\ \hline 3762 \end{array}$

16 $\begin{array}{r} 255 \\ \times\ 718 \\ \hline 283090 \end{array}$

17
$$\begin{array}{r} 5 \\ \times\ 15289 \\ \hline \end{array}$$
76545

18
$$\begin{array}{r} 427 \\ \times\ 489 \\ \hline \end{array}$$

19
$$\begin{array}{r} 31 \\ \times\ 49 \\ \hline \end{array}$$

20
$$\begin{array}{r} 75 \\ \times\ 25 \\ \hline \end{array}$$

21
$$\begin{array}{r} 25 \\ \times\ 25 \\ \hline \end{array}$$

22
$$\begin{array}{r} 49 \\ \times\ 7 \\ \hline \end{array}$$

23
$$\begin{array}{r} 425 \\ \times\ 17 \\ \hline \end{array}$$

24
$$\begin{array}{r} 52 \\ \times\ 78 \\ \hline \end{array}$$

25
$$\begin{array}{r} 310 \\ \times\ 222 \\ \hline \end{array}$$

26
$$\begin{array}{r} 13 \\ \times\ 13 \\ \hline \end{array}$$

27
$$\begin{array}{r} 21 \\ \times\ 63 \\ \hline \end{array}$$

28
$$\begin{array}{r} 45 \\ \times\ 913 \\ \hline \end{array}$$

29
$$\begin{array}{r} 1111 \\ \times\ 33 \\ \hline \end{array}$$

30
$$\begin{array}{r} 54 \\ \times\ 781 \\ \hline \end{array}$$

31
$$\begin{array}{r} 333 \\ \times\ 303 \\ \hline \end{array}$$

32
$$\begin{array}{r} 47 \\ \times\ 23 \\ \hline \end{array}$$

33 The local produce store received an order for 75 bags of potatoes. 30 potatoes can fit into each bag. How many potatoes will the store need to fill the bags?

_____

34 Steven is organizing his stamp collection into large envelopes. He plans to place 60 stamps in each envelope. If he can fill 22 envelopes, how many stamps are in Steven's stamp collection?

_____

Estimating Products

What if you want just a *pretty good* idea of the product?

Is that more or less than the real product? You do not know, because you rounded 515 *downward* and you rounded 39 *upward*. If you round both numbers *upward*, your estimate will be *greater* than the real product. And if you round both numbers *downward*, your estimate will be *less* than the real product.

Example: 39 × 58

That rounds to 40 × 60 = 2400. That product is definitely *greater* than the real product because you rounded both numbers *upward*.

Exercises   ESTIMATE

1 34 × 71

2 456 × 33

3 47 × 67

4 731 × 55

5 78 × 357

6 129 × 157

7 323 × 489

8 417 × 37

9 53 × 49

10 515 × 79

11 745 × 821

12 475 × 71

13 2701 × 23

14 77 × 74

15 521 × 555

16 303 × 251

17 727 × 462

18 92 × 177

19 42 × 420

20 499 × 55

Name _____

Dividing Whole Numbers

Do you work a division problem differently than an addition, subtraction, or multiplication problem? Yes. In division, you work from left to right, *not* from right to left!

To understand what that means, you have to learn some terms used in division. The number to be divided is called the **dividend**. The number that goes into the dividend is called the **divisor**. The answer is called the **quotient**. It shows the number of times the divisor goes into the dividend. Whatever is left over when you're finished is called the **remainder**.

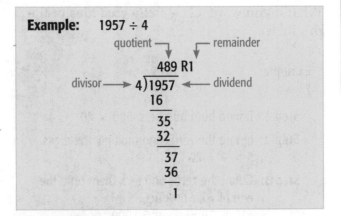

Example: 1957 ÷ 4

Remember...
Your remainder must be *less* than the divisor. `If it is not, go back and check your work.

Exercises DIVIDE

1 7)395

2 21)950

3 12)9475

4 36)18980

5 13)8317

6 44)2000

7 3)256

8 22)801

9 14)788

10 16)15412

11 41)40477

12 37)3041

13 45)9503

14 13)477

15 32)4655

16 89)13183

17 7)4442

18 11)10602

19 14)13501

20 32)1444

21 38)2983

22 3)257

23 11)1039

24 33)1484

25 41)2677

26 8)733

27 12)166

28 74)11616

29 A tailor can repair about 20 garments in a day. How many days will it take him to repair 300 garments?

_____

30 Ms. Bailey is making information packets for all attendees at an education seminar. Each packet contains a total of 28 pages. If Ms. Bailey uses 1,400 sheets of paper, how many people plan to attend the education seminar?

_____

Name _____

Estimating Quotients

What if you need only a *fairly good* idea of a quotient?

You do not use rounding to estimate a quotient. Instead, you find **compatible numbers**, numbers that you can work with easily in your head.

Example: 41297 ÷ 5

Step 1: Look at the two highest digits in the dividend, 41. This cannot be evenly divided by 5, so you will round to the closest compatible number, 40.

Step 2: 40 ÷ 5 = 8

Step 3: Add placeholder zeros to the estimated quotient for the place values you ignored in the original dividend.

41297 ÷ 5 is about 8000

Exercises   ESTIMATE

1. 456 ÷ 8

2. 2112 ÷ 11

3. 674 ÷ 8

4. 4657 ÷ 15

5. 35734 ÷ 12

6. 4252 ÷ 9

7. 67891 ÷ 16

8. 321 ÷ 19

9. 682 ÷ 35

10. 92099 ÷ 34

11. 678 ÷ 22

12. 6578 ÷ 34

13. 789 ÷ 28

14. 4591 ÷ 17

15. 7777 ÷ 44

16. 456 ÷ 7

17. 96291 ÷ 31

18. 91111 ÷ 47

19. 69103 ÷ 41

20. 13401 ÷ 11

Lessons 1–3

Add or subtract.

1   266
    + 45

2   447
    + 58

3   1285
    + 288

4   4339
    + 567

5   639089
    + 13487

6   887
    − 49

7   1468
    − 249

8   6539
    − 144

9   5882
    − 993

10   943
    − 564

Round to the highest place value, then add or subtract.

11   6234
    + 14788

12   24573
    + 29358

13   12661
    44867
    + 9059

14   15768
    44903
    + 9693

15   79255
    5828
    + 4770

16   487
    − 294

17   1765
    − 376

18   28735350
    − 18472

19   22908
    − 11192

20   93556
    − 55690

Lessons 1-3

Multiply or divide.

21
$$\begin{array}{r} 168 \\ \times\ 19 \\ \hline \end{array}$$

22
$$\begin{array}{r} 276 \\ \times\ 81 \\ \hline \end{array}$$

23
$$\begin{array}{r} 874 \\ \times\ 25 \\ \hline \end{array}$$

24
$$\begin{array}{r} 445 \\ \times\ 68 \\ \hline \end{array}$$

25
$$\begin{array}{r} 659 \\ \times\ 74 \\ \hline \end{array}$$

26 $19\overline{)266}$ **27** $24\overline{)504}$ **28** $16\overline{)932}$ **29** $36\overline{)661}$ **30** $71\overline{)948}$

Round to the highest place value, then multiply or divide.

31
$$\begin{array}{r} 918 \\ \times\ 84 \\ \hline \end{array}$$

32
$$\begin{array}{r} 9604 \\ \times\ 31 \\ \hline \end{array}$$

33
$$\begin{array}{r} 77453 \\ \times\ 284 \\ \hline \end{array}$$

34
$$\begin{array}{r} 13845 \\ \times\ 366 \\ \hline \end{array}$$

35
$$\begin{array}{r} 79867 \\ \times\ 578 \\ \hline \end{array}$$

36 $124\overline{)383}$ **37** $175\overline{)1025}$ **38** $95\overline{)1585}$ **39** $73\overline{)8898}$ **40** $96\overline{)98455}$

Lessons 1–3

Give the place value of the number 7 for questions 41–44.

41 1,845,732   **42** 45.357   **43** 73,561,132.001   **44** 20.075

_____   _____   _____   _____

45 Parks Commissioner Davis is planning for the town's upcoming fiscal year. Last year the town had a total of 2,435 visitors to its nature center, 7,693 visitors to its children's park, and 9,287 visitors to its arboretum. How many visitors did the town's parks have, in total, last year?

_____

46 Last year Trey had 435 coins in his collection. This year Trey added 124 more coins to his collection. How many coins does he now have in his collection?

_____

47 Edie's favorite magazine has a total of 1,476 pages of advertising each year. If the magazine is published every month, about how many pages of advertising are in each issue?

_____

How many pages exactly?

_____

48 At 1,776 feet in height, the new Freedom Tower in New York will be one of the tallest buildings in the world. What is the height of the building written in expanded form?

_____

49 What is the word form of the number 19,238,976?

_____

_____

50 The United States Post Office delivers 668 million pieces of mail each day to over 142 million delivery points. How many pieces of mail does the Post Office deliver in a year? (Assume there are 312 delivery days in a year.)

_____

What is that in expanded form?

_____

_____

Name _____

Changing Improper Fractions to Mixed Numbers

What words must you know to talk about fractions? You have to know that the number on the bottom is the **denominator**, which tells what kind of units the whole is divided into. The number on the top is the **numerator**, which tells how many of those units there are.

A fraction is less than 1 when the numerator is less than the denominator. A fraction is equal to 1 when the numerator is the same as the denominator. A fraction is *greater* than 1 when the numerator is greater than the denominator. Any fraction greater than 1 is an **improper fraction**. It can be changed into a **mixed number**, which is part whole number and part fraction.

Example: Change $\frac{13}{4}$ to a mixed number.
Step 1: $13 \div 4 = 3\,R1$
So $\frac{13}{4} = 3\frac{1}{4}$

Exercises   CHANGE TO MIXED NUMBERS

1 $\frac{44}{3}$

2 $\frac{91}{4}$

3 $\frac{5}{2}$

4 $\frac{22}{3}$

5 $\frac{55}{12}$

6 $\frac{107}{11}$

7 $\frac{156}{16}$

8 $\frac{31}{8}$

9 $\frac{101}{21}$

10 $\frac{33}{2}$

11 $\frac{47}{11}$

12 $\frac{202}{19}$

13 $\frac{78}{8}$

14 $\frac{47}{7}$

15 $\frac{147}{12}$

16 $\frac{260}{16}$

17 $\frac{58}{3}$

18 $\frac{77}{4}$

19 $\frac{133}{12}$

20 $\frac{345}{7}$

Changing Mixed Numbers to Improper Fractions

You know that you can change an improper fraction to a mixed number. You can also change a mixed number into an improper fraction. First, multiply the whole number by the denominator of the fraction. Then, add the numerator to that product. Finally, place the total over the denominator.

Example: Change $8\frac{3}{5}$ into an improper fraction

Step 1: $8 \times 5 = 40$

Step 2: $40 + 3 = 43$ So $8\frac{3}{5} = \frac{43}{5}$

Exercises   CHANGE TO IMPROPER FRACTIONS

1 $3\frac{1}{4}$

2 $5\frac{3}{7}$

3 $12\frac{3}{11}$

4 $14\frac{3}{5}$

5 $1\frac{2}{13}$

6 $21\frac{3}{14}$

7 $33\frac{1}{9}$

8 $4\frac{1}{17}$

9 $102\frac{1}{7}$

10 $32\frac{1}{2}$

11 $29\frac{1}{29}$

12 $37\frac{3}{8}$

13 $15\frac{2}{3}$

14 $61\frac{5}{14}$

15 $7\frac{2}{17}$

16 $6\frac{3}{22}$

17 $23\frac{2}{3}$

18 $15\frac{4}{7}$

19 $13\frac{1}{13}$

20 $4\frac{4}{44}$

Name _____

Adding Fractions with Like Denominators

Can you add fractions that have the same denominator? Two denominators that are exactly the same are called **like denominators**. They are easy to add, because you can ignore the denominators when adding!

Example: $\frac{5}{9} + \frac{2}{9}$

Step 1: Add the numerators. $5 + 2 = 7$

Step 2: Place the total over the like denominator. So $\frac{5}{9} + \frac{2}{9} = \frac{7}{9}$

Exercises   ADD

1 $\frac{1}{2} + \frac{1}{2}$

2 $\frac{4}{5} + \frac{3}{5}$

3 $\frac{7}{8} + \frac{3}{8}$

4 $\frac{6}{7} + \frac{2}{7}$

5 $\frac{10}{11} + \frac{14}{11}$

6 $\frac{71}{17} + \frac{3}{17}$

7 $\frac{4}{9} + \frac{34}{9}$

8 $\frac{2}{3} + \frac{7}{3}$

9 $\begin{array}{r} \frac{4}{23} \\ + \frac{54}{23} \end{array}$

10 $\begin{array}{r} \frac{3}{37} \\ + \frac{54}{37} \end{array}$

11 $\begin{array}{r} \frac{3}{4} \\ + \frac{5}{4} \end{array}$

12 $\begin{array}{r} \frac{7}{11} \\ + \frac{5}{11} \end{array}$

13 $\begin{array}{r} \frac{5}{27} \\ + \frac{10}{27} \end{array}$

14 $\begin{array}{r} \frac{3}{4} \\ + \frac{13}{4} \end{array}$

15 $\begin{array}{r} \frac{23}{24} \\ + \frac{19}{24} \end{array}$

16 $\begin{array}{r} \frac{3}{37} \\ + \frac{10}{37} \end{array}$

Subtracting Fractions with Like Denominators

Do you use the same kind of process to subtract fractions with like denominators? Yes, exactly! Ignore the denominator when doing your work.

To add or subtract fractions with like denominators, you only need to work with the numerators. Don't forget to put your total or difference over the same denominator.

Example: $\frac{14}{17} - \frac{9}{17}$

Step 1: $14 - 9 = 5$

So $\frac{14}{17} - \frac{9}{17} = \frac{5}{17}$

Exercises   SUBTRACT

1 $\frac{3}{4} - \frac{1}{4}$

2 $\frac{7}{8} - \frac{5}{8}$

3 $\frac{7}{4} - \frac{1}{4}$

4 $\frac{14}{5} - \frac{8}{5}$

5 $\frac{33}{7} - \frac{29}{7}$

6 $\frac{9}{11} - \frac{7}{11}$

7 $\frac{14}{3} - \frac{7}{3}$

8 $\frac{21}{19} - \frac{13}{19}$

9 $\frac{12}{5}$
$- \frac{2}{5}$

10 $\frac{23}{7}$
$- \frac{17}{7}$

11 $\frac{45}{8}$
$- \frac{37}{8}$

12 $\frac{12}{51}$
$- \frac{4}{51}$

13 $\frac{43}{13}$
$- \frac{14}{13}$

14 $\frac{56}{17}$
$- \frac{35}{17}$

15 $\frac{7}{4}$
$- \frac{3}{4}$

16 $\frac{32}{37}$
$- \frac{14}{37}$

Adding or Subtracting Fractions with Unlike Denominators

Can you add or subtract fractions if the denominators are different? Yes you can, but first you have to change your fractions so that they have a **common denominator**. This is another term for like denominator.

When you find a common multiple, take one fraction at a time. Multiply the original denominator to make it become the common denominator, and multiply the numerator by the same number. When you multiply the numerator *and* the denominator of a fraction by the same number, you do *not* change the value of the fraction.

Example: $\frac{5}{8} + \frac{1}{6}$

Step 1: Find a common multiple for both denominators. 24

Step 2: Multiply both the numerator and the denominator by the number that will make the denominator equal the common multiple. Do this for both fractions.

$$\frac{5}{8} = \frac{5 \times 3}{8 \times 3} \qquad \frac{1}{6} = \frac{4 \times 1}{4 \times 6}$$

Step 3: Add the fractions. $\frac{15}{24} + \frac{4}{24} = \frac{19}{24}$

Remember...

Once you find a common denominator, the calculations are easy!

Exercises   **ADD OR SUBTRACT**

1 $\frac{1}{4} + \frac{1}{5}$ **2** $\frac{2}{7} + \frac{2}{3}$ **3** $\frac{21}{20} + \frac{1}{3}$ **4** $\frac{12}{13} - \frac{1}{2}$ **5** $\frac{3}{4} - \frac{1}{7}$

6 $\frac{23}{21} + \frac{1}{5}$ **7** $\frac{32}{11} - \frac{2}{3}$ **8** $\frac{12}{7} + \frac{2}{3}$ **9** $\frac{8}{15} - \frac{1}{3}$ **10** $\frac{7}{8} - \frac{2}{5}$

11 $\begin{array}{r} \frac{54}{11} \\ + \frac{2}{7} \end{array}$ **12** $\begin{array}{r} \frac{13}{12} \\ - \frac{4}{5} \end{array}$ **13** $\begin{array}{r} \frac{56}{13} \\ - \frac{2}{3} \end{array}$ **14** $\begin{array}{r} \frac{3}{4} \\ - \frac{2}{5} \end{array}$ **15** $\begin{array}{r} \frac{21}{4} \\ - \frac{5}{2} \end{array}$

Adding Mixed Numbers with Unlike Denominators

How do you add mixed numbers with unlike denominators? There are *two* ways to do this. In both ways, you will have to find a common denominator for the fractions.

One way is to change each mixed number to an improper fraction, then find the common denominator and add the fractions. The other way is even simpler. Just add the whole number parts first. Then find the common denominator for the fractions and add the fractions. Add the total fraction to your total whole number.

Example: $3\frac{2}{3} + 6\frac{1}{2}$

Step 1: Add the whole numbers. $3 + 6 = 9$

Step 2: Find a common denominator for the fractions. $\frac{2}{3} = \frac{4}{6}$ and $\frac{1}{2} = \frac{3}{6}$

Step 3: Add the fractions. $\frac{4}{6} + \frac{3}{6} = \frac{7}{6} = 1\frac{1}{6}$

Step 4: Add the sum of the fractions to the sum of the whole numbers.

$3\frac{2}{3} + 6\frac{1}{2} = 9 + 1\frac{1}{6} = 10\frac{1}{6}$

Exercises ADD MIXED NUMBERS

1 $2\frac{1}{2} + 3\frac{1}{4}$

2 $3\frac{2}{3} + 4\frac{3}{7}$

3 $4\frac{5}{6} + 7\frac{3}{4}$

4 $3\frac{3}{4} + 2\frac{1}{3}$

5 $9\frac{1}{2} + 4\frac{1}{5}$

6 $54\frac{1}{2} + 14\frac{2}{3}$

7 $10\frac{5}{7} + 12\frac{2}{3}$

8 $4\frac{2}{9} + 3\frac{2}{7}$

9 $13\frac{4}{5} + 4\frac{3}{11}$

10 $23\frac{1}{6} + 57\frac{3}{13}$

11 $22\frac{3}{11} + 14\frac{2}{5}$

12 $4\frac{5}{7} + 3\frac{1}{3}$

13 $\quad 5\frac{1}{4}$
$+ \quad 7\frac{2}{15}$
_____

14 $\quad 102\frac{5}{6}$
$+ \quad 355\frac{1}{11}$
_____

15 $\quad 56\frac{1}{3}$
$+ \quad 89\frac{5}{14}$
_____

16 $\quad 21\frac{1}{2}$
$+ \quad 122\frac{3}{8}$
_____

Subtracting Mixed Numbers with Unlike Denominators

How do you subtract mixed numbers with unlike denominators? You do the same thing you do when you add mixed numbers with unlike denominators. You find a common denominator for the fractions.

Example: $12\frac{5}{7} - 9\frac{2}{5}$

Step 1: Subtract the whole numbers. $12 - 9 = 3$

Step 2: Find a common denominator for the fractions. $\frac{5}{7} = \frac{25}{35}$ and $\frac{2}{5} = \frac{14}{35}$

Step 3: Subtract the fractions. $\frac{25}{35} - \frac{14}{35} = \frac{11}{35}$

Step 4: *Add* the difference of the fractions to the difference of the whole numbers.

$3 + \frac{11}{35} = 3\frac{11}{35}$

If the difference in step 3 is less than zero, then you *will subtract* that number from the difference of the whole numbers.

Exercises   SUBTRACT MIXED NUMBERS

1 $5\frac{1}{2} - 2\frac{1}{4}$

2 $10\frac{3}{7} - 4\frac{2}{11}$

3 $21\frac{5}{9} - 4\frac{2}{5}$

4 $13\frac{5}{6} - 10\frac{2}{9}$

5 $14\frac{2}{3} - 5\frac{1}{6}$

6 $21\frac{3}{4} - 11\frac{5}{9}$

7 $13\frac{5}{6} - 3\frac{1}{7}$

8 $43\frac{4}{5} - 29\frac{3}{11}$

9 $\begin{array}{r} 10\frac{6}{11} \\ - 4\frac{1}{2} \\ \hline \end{array}$

10 $\begin{array}{r} 13\frac{2}{3} \\ - 11\frac{5}{9} \\ \hline \end{array}$

11 $\begin{array}{r} 77\frac{2}{3} \\ - 41\frac{2}{17} \\ \hline \end{array}$

12 $\begin{array}{r} 19\frac{5}{7} \\ - 3\frac{1}{14} \\ \hline \end{array}$

13 Janelle practiced playing the piano $2\frac{1}{2}$ hours on Saturday. On Sunday, she practiced for $3\frac{1}{4}$ hours. How many more hours did Janelle practice on Sunday than on Saturday?

_____

14 Robby is helping his father make a casserole for dinner. They purchased $1\frac{1}{4}$ pounds of potatoes, and used $\frac{2}{3}$ pounds of potatoes to make one casserole. Do they have enough potatoes left over to make the casserole a second time?

_____

Estimating Sums and Differences of Fractions and Mixed Numbers

FRACTIONS What if you only need a *fairly good idea* of the sum or difference of some fractions?

Example: Estimate $\frac{4}{7} + \frac{9}{10} + \frac{1}{16}$

Step 1: Round each fraction to the nearest half number and complete the problem.

$$\frac{1}{2} + 1 + 0 = 1\frac{1}{2}$$

MIXED NUMBERS Can you estimate subtraction of mixed numbers, too? Of course! First, estimate the difference of the whole numbers.

Then estimate the difference of the fractions. Add your two estimates together.

Example: Estimate $62\frac{15}{16} - 28\frac{4}{7}$

Step 1: Estimate the difference of the whole numbers. $60 - 30 = 30$

Step 2: Estimate the difference of the fractions.
$$1 - \frac{1}{2} = \frac{1}{2}$$

Step 3: Add the difference of the fractions to the difference of the whole numbers.
$62\frac{15}{16} - 28\frac{4}{7}$ is about $30\frac{1}{2}$

Exercises ESTIMATE SUMS AND DIFFERENCES

1 $12\frac{5}{8} + 23\frac{5}{6}$

2 $57\frac{2}{3} + 34\frac{5}{8}$

3 $81\frac{1}{8} + 29\frac{4}{5}$

4 $202\frac{1}{9} - 34\frac{3}{9}$

5 $5501\frac{3}{4} - 456\frac{3}{5}$

6 $457\frac{8}{13} - 98\frac{8}{13}$

7 $67\frac{4}{19} + 53\frac{9}{23}$

8 $189\frac{4}{5} + 321\frac{6}{7}$

9 $547\frac{17}{19} - 44\frac{4}{11}$

10 $49\frac{5}{6} + 51\frac{1}{7}$

11 $67\frac{2}{3} + 46\frac{9}{23}$

12 $456\frac{6}{7} - 145\frac{5}{14}$

13 James has $32\frac{1}{8}$ ounces of dog food. If he feeds each of his three dogs $6\frac{3}{4}$ ounces of food, about how much dog food will be left?

_____

14 Sherry is making cookies for her family's holiday gift baskets. She has already made $5\frac{1}{4}$ dozen cookies. If Sherry makes an additional $3\frac{1}{2}$ dozen cookies, about how many dozen cookies will go into the gift baskets?

_____

Name _____

Multiplying Fractions and Whole Numbers

Is there a simple way to multiply a fraction by a whole number? Yes. Multiply the fraction's *numerator* by the whole number. Then write that product over the fraction's denominator. If the final fraction is an improper fraction, you may need to change it to a mixed number.

Example: $17 \times \frac{2}{3}$

Step 1: Multiply the whole number by the numerator. Place your answer over the denominator. $\frac{17 \times 2}{3} = \frac{34}{3}$

Step 2: Change your answer to a mixed number. $\frac{34}{3} = 11\frac{1}{3}$

Exercises MULTIPLY

1. $3 \times \frac{1}{4}$

2. $15 \times \frac{2}{7}$

3. $12 \times \frac{3}{8}$

4. $22 \times \frac{3}{11}$

5. $15 \times \frac{3}{20}$

6. $31 \times \frac{2}{17}$

7. $6 \times \frac{7}{24}$

8. $14 \times \frac{10}{11}$

9. $16 \times \frac{5}{36}$

10. $7 \times \frac{2}{3}$

11. $16 \times \frac{3}{5}$

12. $11 \times \frac{11}{12}$

13. $42 \times \frac{5}{7}$

14. $20 \times \frac{3}{40}$

15. $32 \times \frac{5}{8}$

16. $15 \times \frac{1}{15}$

17. $16 \times \frac{3}{16}$

18. $3 \times \frac{1}{3}$

19. $45 \times \frac{13}{15}$

20. $7 \times \frac{4}{7}$

Multiplying Fractions; Reciprocals

Is it complicated to multiply two fractions? No, it is easy if you know how to multiply whole numbers. Just multiply the numerators to get the numerator of the product. Then multiply the denominators to get the denominator of the product.

If the fractions are **reciprocals**, you do not even have to multiply at all! Reciprocals are two fractions that look like each other upside-down. The numerator of the first is the denominator of the second and the numerator of the second is the denominator of the first.

The product of reciprocals is *always* 1.

Example: $\frac{3}{5} \times \frac{8}{9}$

Step 1: Multiply the numerators and the denominators. $3 \times 8 = 24$, $5 \times 9 = 45$

Step 2: $\frac{3}{5} \times \frac{8}{9} = \frac{24}{45}$

Examples:

$\frac{2}{3} \times \frac{3}{2} = 1$ $\frac{43}{50} \times \frac{50}{43} = 1$ $\frac{987}{106} \times \frac{106}{987} = 1$

Exercises MULTIPLY

1. $\frac{1}{2} \times \frac{2}{3}$

2. $\frac{5}{7} \times \frac{3}{8}$

3. $\frac{20}{21} \times \frac{2}{5}$

4. $\frac{3}{2} \times \frac{3}{2}$

5. $\frac{2}{3} \times \frac{3}{2}$

6. $\frac{7}{4} \times \frac{16}{3}$

7. $\frac{5}{9} \times \frac{90}{10}$

8. $\frac{4}{7} \times \frac{3}{28}$

9. $\frac{3}{11} \times \frac{11}{3}$

10. $\frac{12}{13} \times \frac{39}{2}$

11. $\frac{3}{8} \times \frac{2}{13}$

12. $\frac{7}{8} \times \frac{16}{3}$

13. $\frac{81}{7} \times \frac{1}{9}$

14. $\frac{7}{3} \times \frac{3}{14}$

15. $\frac{15}{16} \times \frac{3}{5}$

16. $\frac{10}{13} \times \frac{52}{7}$

Multiplying Mixed Numbers; Reducing

How do you multiply mixed numbers? Change each mixed number into an improper fraction, then multiply the fractions.

Many fractions can be reduced. **Reducing** changes a fraction into its simplest form. To reduce, find a number that divides evenly into both the numerator and denominator. Then divide *both* the numerator and the denominator by that number. In Step 2 of the example, both the numerator and the denominator of the multiplication product can be divided evenly by 5. You don't always have to wait until you finish multiplying to reduce. Sometimes you

can reduce *before* you multiply. If you are multiplying two fractions, look at both numerators and then at both denominators. If you can divide *either* numerator by the same number as *either* denominator, you can reduce.

Example: $1\frac{7}{10} \times 3\frac{3}{4}$

Step 1: $1\frac{7}{10} = \frac{17}{10}, \ 3\frac{3}{4} = \frac{15}{4}$

Step 2: $\frac{17}{10} \times \frac{15}{4} = \frac{255}{40} = \frac{51}{8} = 6\frac{3}{8}$

Exercises MULTIPLY

1 $5\frac{1}{4} \times \frac{1}{2}$

2 $\frac{1}{3} \times 5\frac{1}{3}$

3 $12\frac{1}{4} \times \frac{3}{2}$

4 $3\frac{1}{7} \times \frac{14}{3}$

5 $\frac{1}{5} \times 1\frac{3}{4}$

6 $6\frac{5}{7} \times \frac{2}{3}$

7 $4\frac{2}{5} \times \frac{3}{8}$

8 $3\frac{1}{4} \times \frac{5}{8}$

9 $3\frac{2}{5} \times \frac{5}{9}$

10 $\frac{1}{4} \times 4\frac{1}{3}$

11 $3\frac{2}{3} \times 1\frac{2}{7}$

12 $4\frac{1}{5} \times 2\frac{3}{14}$

13 $5\frac{1}{4} \times 3\frac{1}{3}$

14 $2\frac{4}{5} \times 4\frac{2}{7}$

15 $3\frac{3}{4} \times 3\frac{3}{10}$

16 $3\frac{1}{3} \times 3\frac{3}{5}$

Dividing Fractions by Whole Numbers

To divide a fraction by a whole number, multiply the denominator by the whole number.

Example: $\frac{7}{9} \div 3$

Step 1: Multiply the whole number by the denominator. $9 \times 3 = 27$

Step 2: Place the numerator over the product.
$$\frac{7}{9} \div 3 = \frac{7}{27}$$

Exercises DIVIDE

1 $\frac{1}{2} \div 4$

2 $\frac{3}{5} \div 4$

3 $\frac{6}{7} \div 3$

4 $\frac{1}{5} \div 11$

5 $\frac{5}{19} \div 2$

6 $\frac{4}{5} \div 7$

7 $\frac{1}{9} \div 9$

8 $\frac{3}{11} \div 12$

9 $\frac{17}{18} \div 4$

10 $\frac{12}{13} \div 3$

11 $\frac{2}{3} \div 6$

12 $\frac{5}{11} \div 20$

13 $\frac{3}{7} \div 11$

14 $\frac{1}{3} \div 9$

15 $\frac{10}{11} \div 5$

16 $\frac{10}{13} \div 4$

17 $\frac{4}{5} \div 4$

18 $\frac{12}{13} \div 5$

19 $\frac{2}{11} \div 4$

20 $\frac{3}{4} \div 7$

Dividing Whole Numbers by Fractions

Why do you multiply to divide a whole number by a fraction? Actually, to divide a whole number by a fraction, you multiply the whole number by the reciprocal of the fraction.

Example: $5 \div \frac{2}{3}$

Step 1: Multiply the whole number by the reciprocal of the fraction.

$$5 \times \frac{3}{2} = \frac{15}{2} = 7\frac{1}{2}$$

Exercises | **DIVIDE**

① $5 \div \frac{1}{4}$

② $3 \div \frac{4}{5}$

③ $7 \div \frac{1}{7}$

④ $9 \div \frac{4}{7}$

⑤ $2 \div \frac{1}{2}$

⑥ $4 \div \frac{2}{7}$

⑦ $15 \div \frac{5}{7}$

⑧ $4 \div \frac{2}{9}$

⑨ $17 \div \frac{2}{3}$

⑩ $5 \div \frac{3}{5}$

⑪ $6 \div \frac{2}{3}$

⑫ $9 \div \frac{2}{3}$

⑬ $5 \div \frac{1}{11}$

⑭ $14 \div \frac{7}{2}$

⑮ $3 \div \frac{1}{9}$

⑯ $3 \div \frac{7}{2}$

Name _____

Dividing Fractions by Fractions

How do you divide a fraction by another fraction? Can you multiply by a reciprocal in that kind of problem? Yes! You multiply the first fraction by the reciprocal of the second.

Example: $\dfrac{3}{10} \div \dfrac{2}{3}$

$$\dfrac{3}{10} \times \dfrac{3}{2} = \dfrac{9}{20}$$

Exercises DIVIDE

1 $\dfrac{5}{7} \div \dfrac{3}{4}$

2 $\dfrac{2}{3} \div \dfrac{2}{7}$

3 $\dfrac{1}{9} \div \dfrac{3}{7}$

4 $\dfrac{3}{4} \div \dfrac{1}{9}$

5 $\dfrac{3}{13} \div \dfrac{2}{9}$

6 $\dfrac{1}{9} \div \dfrac{1}{3}$

7 $\dfrac{2}{13} \div \dfrac{1}{5}$

8 $\dfrac{3}{13} \div \dfrac{2}{13}$

9 $\dfrac{4}{3} \div \dfrac{1}{4}$

10 $\dfrac{15}{4} \div \dfrac{4}{3}$

11 $\dfrac{6}{7} \div \dfrac{1}{7}$

12 $\dfrac{3}{17} \div \dfrac{4}{17}$

13 $\dfrac{1}{11} \div \dfrac{22}{3}$

14 $\dfrac{3}{7} \div \dfrac{1}{21}$

15 $\dfrac{5}{14} \div \dfrac{1}{7}$

16 $\dfrac{3}{4} \div \dfrac{8}{3}$

6.4

Dividing Mixed Numbers

How can you use a reciprocal to divide a mixed number by another mixed number? A mixed number can be changed into an improper fraction. So change both mixed numbers into improper fractions. Then multiply the first fraction by the reciprocal of the second.

Remember...

Do not forget to simplify if you can. If necessary, change your answer from an improper fraction back to a mixed number.

Example: $3\frac{3}{5} \div 2\frac{3}{6}$

Step 1: Change to improper fractions.
$3\frac{2}{5} = \frac{18}{5}$, $2\frac{3}{6} = \frac{15}{6}$

Step 2: Multiply the first fraction by the reciprocal of the second. $\frac{18}{5} \times \frac{6}{15}$

Step 3: $18 \times 6 = 108$, $5 \times 15 = 75$

Step 4: Reduce your answer and convert to a mixed number. $\frac{108}{75} = \frac{36}{25} = 1\frac{11}{25}$

Exercises   DIVIDE

1 $1\frac{1}{3} \div 2\frac{1}{2}$

2 $3\frac{3}{5} \div 1\frac{1}{8}$

3 $7\frac{1}{7} \div 3\frac{1}{3}$

4 $3\frac{4}{7} \div 2\frac{2}{5}$

5 $6\frac{4}{5} \div 3\frac{2}{5}$

6 $5\frac{1}{2} \div 3\frac{3}{4}$

7 $4\frac{2}{9} \div 2\frac{4}{9}$

8 $9\frac{2}{7} \div 2\frac{1}{2}$

9 $5\frac{6}{17} \div 2\frac{2}{3}$

10 $5\frac{3}{13} \div 2\frac{3}{4}$

11 $1\frac{3}{4} \div 4\frac{3}{5}$

12 $9\frac{3}{8} \div 1\frac{1}{4}$

13 $44\frac{4}{5} \div 4\frac{1}{2}$

14 $1\frac{1}{2} \div 3\frac{1}{2}$

15 $5\frac{3}{5} \div 1\frac{1}{3}$

16 $1\frac{2}{11} \div 3\frac{1}{3}$

Ratios

A **ratio**, often expressed as a fraction, compares two numbers.

Examples:

Eight people want equal shares of one pie. You can set up a ratio.

$$\frac{1 \text{ pie}}{8 \text{ people}}$$

When you remove the words, you can see that each person should get $\frac{1}{8}$ of the pie. The ratio of pie to people is 1:8

You can compare *any* two numbers with a ratio. For example: Kira read 5 books last month, and Carmen read 4.

$$\frac{5 \text{ Kira books}}{4 \text{ Carmen books}}$$

The ratio of Kira's reading to Carmen's reading was 5:4 (Say "five to four"). You can also express that as a mixed number. Kira read $1\frac{1}{4}$ times as many books as Carmen.

Exercises   COMPARE

1. Jennifer is making a cake that requires 2 cups of flour and 1 cup of milk. What is the ratio of flour to milk?

_____

2. At the movie theatre the manager wants to know which movie is selling the most tickets. He finds that movie A sold 150 tickets and movie B sold 100 tickets. What is the ratio of sales? Reduce your answer.

_____

3. Judy and Nancy have been swimming at the pool for one hour a day for the last month. Judy averages 25 laps every hour while Nancy averages 18. What is the ratio of laps they swam?

_____

4. Michael and Leon get ice cream cones, Michael orders chocolate chip and Leon orders yogurt chips. They each count the number of chocolate chips and yogurt chips that they eat until they finish. Michael had 32 and Leon 17. What is the ratio of yogurt chips to chocolate chips in the ice cream?

_____

5. Joshua and Steve are erecting a fence around a pasture. Each day Steve erects 200 feet of fence while Joshua erects 150 feet. What is the ratio of work that Steve completes versus Joshua?

_____

Name _____

Proportions and Cross-Multiplying

Do you ever have to use more than one ratio to solve a problem? Yes. A **proportion** is a problem that contains two ratios that are equal. You set up a proportion problem when you do not know the value of one of the numerators or one of the denominators. This kind of problem is called an **equation**. An equation is a mathematical statement that two things are equal. In this example, q stands for the unknown number of *quarts*. Let's say that you are giving a party for 20 people. You know that two quarts of potato salad will be enough for 10 people.

Cross-multiplying is the way to find the missing number. Multiply the numerator of the first fraction by the denominator of the second fraction and write the product on one side of the equation. Then muliply the denominator of the first fraction by the numerator of the second fraction and write that product on the other side of the equation. To get the answer, look at the side that has both a known number and the unknown number. Divide *both* sides of the equation by that known number.

Remember...

If you divide both sides of an equation by the *same* number, they will still be equal.

Example: $\dfrac{2 \text{ quarts}}{10 \text{ people}} = \dfrac{\text{(how many quarts?)}}{20 \text{ people}}$

Step 1: Set up your equation. $\dfrac{2}{10} = \dfrac{q}{20}$

Step 2: Cross-multiply. $40 = 10q$

$4 = q$

Exercises   CROSS-MULTIPLY

Round to the hundredths place.

1. $\dfrac{x}{5} = \dfrac{30}{15}$

2. $\dfrac{z}{3} = \dfrac{24}{6}$

3. $\dfrac{14}{z} = \dfrac{100}{50}$

4. $\dfrac{56}{4} = \dfrac{y}{20}$

5. $\dfrac{45}{9} = \dfrac{w}{3}$

6. $\dfrac{14}{x} = \dfrac{70}{10}$

7. $\dfrac{33}{r} = \dfrac{11}{3}$

8. $\dfrac{72}{9} = \dfrac{24}{z}$

9. $\dfrac{3}{2} = \dfrac{x}{5}$

10. $\dfrac{700}{50} = \dfrac{35}{w}$

11. $\dfrac{36}{4} = \dfrac{x}{6}$

12. $\dfrac{84}{12} = \dfrac{q}{4}$

Rates

What other kinds of problems can using proportions help you solve? Proportions can be used to solve a rate problem.

When you set up the equation, be sure that the numerators are the same units and the denominators are the same units. In this equation, the numerators are blocks and the denominators are minutes.

Example:

Your friend Becky can ride her bike at the rate of 6 blocks in 5 minutes. How many minutes will it take her to ride 30 blocks?

$$\frac{6}{5} = \frac{30}{m}$$

$6m = 150$

$m = 25$

Exercises   SOLVE

1 The two rectangles below are similar (proportional). Given the information about rectangle EFGH, what is the length of side CD?

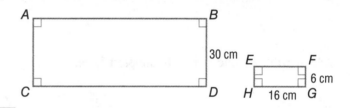

_____

2 George likes to sweeten his ice tea. When he drinks a 20-ounce ice tea he puts in two teaspoons of sugar. If he is making a gallon of ice tea, how many teaspoons of sugar should he add?

_____

3 The two triangles below are similar. Calculate the length of side *s*.

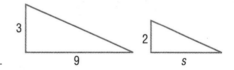

_____

4 Chuck took a long hike where he started at point B and followed the path in the diagram shown. If Chuck wants to take a shorter hike where he starts at B and walks 4 miles east, turns and walks 3 miles north and then returns to point B, how long would his last leg be. Solve this problem using proportions even though you can solve it using the Pythagorean Theorem.

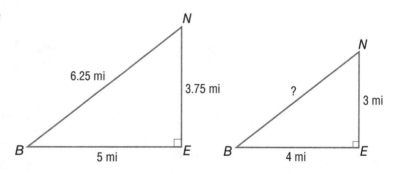

_____

Unit Test

Lessons 4–7

Change to mixed numbers.

1 $\dfrac{17}{7}$

2 $\dfrac{29}{6}$

3 $\dfrac{102}{17}$

4 $\dfrac{350}{33}$

Change to improper fractions.

5 $7\dfrac{6}{11}$

6 $5\dfrac{4}{13}$

7 $4\dfrac{15}{19}$

8 $7\dfrac{7}{16}$

Add or subtract, and reduce to simplest form.

9 $1\dfrac{3}{4}+\dfrac{3}{4}$

10 $\dfrac{17}{49}-\dfrac{11}{49}$

11 $1\dfrac{5}{11}+\dfrac{3}{11}$

12 $2\dfrac{23}{39}+\dfrac{24}{39}$

13 $\dfrac{34}{41}-\dfrac{13}{41}$

14 $\dfrac{11}{32}+\dfrac{19}{32}$

15 $\dfrac{55}{93}-\dfrac{28}{93}$

16 $\dfrac{36}{74}+\dfrac{33}{74}$

17 $5\dfrac{3}{17}-4\dfrac{2}{17}$

18 $4\dfrac{23}{33}+\dfrac{17}{24}$

19 $\dfrac{4}{9}+\dfrac{4}{15}$

20 $\dfrac{14}{25}-\dfrac{13}{35}$

21 $1\dfrac{5}{9}+\dfrac{3}{11}$

22 $1\dfrac{7}{19}-\dfrac{2}{7}$

23 $\dfrac{3}{4}-\dfrac{19}{41}$

24 $2\dfrac{8}{13}+\dfrac{9}{17}$

Lessons 4–7

Estimate, then add or subtract.

25 $2\frac{14}{25} - 1\frac{17}{21}$ **26** $9\frac{22}{63} + 25\frac{43}{63}$ **27** $12\frac{23}{29} + 11\frac{17}{29}$ **28** $18\frac{3}{7} + 5\frac{1}{4}$

Multiply or divide, and reduce to simplest form.

29 $3 \times 3\frac{2}{11}$ **30** $\frac{1}{2} \times 55$ **31** $\frac{3}{4} \times 24$ **32** $\frac{14}{18} \times \frac{11}{28}$

33 $\frac{1}{3} \times 4\frac{7}{9}$ **34** $16 \times \frac{3}{11}$ **35** $\frac{16}{29} \div 48$ **36** $\frac{51}{47} \div 17$

37 $\frac{7}{3} \div 42$ **38** $\frac{4}{27} \div 3$ **39** $\frac{75}{83} \div 15$ **40** $39 \div \frac{6}{7}$

41 $125 \div \frac{25}{44}$ **42** $\frac{3}{4} \div \frac{16}{27}$ **43** $\frac{24}{17} \div \frac{17}{24}$ **44** $\frac{39}{76} \div \frac{52}{57}$

Name _____

Lessons 4–7

Determine if the following proportions are equal. (Write Yes or No)

45 $\dfrac{5}{4} = \dfrac{24}{16}$ _____

46 $\dfrac{21}{12} = \dfrac{7}{36}$ _____

47 $\dfrac{12}{19} = \dfrac{36}{57}$ _____

48 $\dfrac{1}{4} = \dfrac{6}{24}$ _____

Solve for x.

49 $\dfrac{x}{10} = \dfrac{30}{20}$

50 $\dfrac{25}{x} = \dfrac{40}{100}$

51 $\dfrac{33}{96} = \dfrac{11}{x}$

52 $\dfrac{1}{10} = \dfrac{20}{x}$

Solve.

53 Create a ratio to compare the length of the side of a barn (140 ft) to the width of the barn (64 ft). _____

54 Create a ratio to compare the amount of unsaturated fat in salad dressing (5 grams) to the amount of carbohydrates (9 grams). _____

55 Wallace rides his bicycle at an average speed of 18 miles per hour. How many miles does he travel in $3\dfrac{1}{3}$ hours? _____

56 Jermaine can make 29 loaves of bread for every 3 batches he bakes. How many batches of bread does he need to bake in order to make 232 loaves? _____

57 Phyllis drinks $\dfrac{3}{4}$ of a pint of water after each mile she walks. How many pints of water will she drink if she walks $5\dfrac{3}{4}$ miles? _____

58 Ginny needs to check the air in her tires every 750 miles. How many times will she need to check her tires if she is taking a trip that is 6,750 miles in length? _____

Place Value and Rounding

Understanding place value can help you work with decimals.

Look at the chart. Suppose you are asked to round a decimal to its highest whole number. You can do that by looking at the digit in the tenths place. If that digit is less than 5, round to the whole number that is there. If the digit in the tenths place is 5 or greater, add 1 to the whole number.

Tens	Ones		Tenths	Hundredths	Thousandths
1	5	.	4	0	7

You can also round a decimal to its nearest tenth, its nearest hundredth, its nearest thousandth, and so on. Just look at the digit to the *right* of the rounding place. If that digit is less than 5, keep the digit you see in the rounding place. If that digit is 5 or greater, add 1 to the digit in the rounding place.

Exercises ROUND

Round to the nearest whole number.

1 45.7

2 77.4

3 145.6

4 1000.9

5 89.4

6 1501.1

Round to the nearest tenth.

7 14.37

8 125.51

9 149.49

10 33.35

11 275.77

12 212.99

Round to the nearest hundredth.

13 1435.344

14 3.555

15 111.119

16 32.756

17 999.989

18 954.376

Round to the nearest thousandth.

19 3.2378

20 329.3297

21 109.1090

22 8256.7835

23 49.4949

24 0.1138

Name _____

Changing Fractions to Decimals

What is the difference between a decimal and a fraction? Actually, a decimal *is* a fraction. It is just expressed in a different way. So $0.7 = \frac{7}{100}$, and $5.023 = 5\frac{23}{1000}$.

However, decimals are expressed only in tenths, hundredths, thousandths, and so on. So some fractions cannot be converted to simple decimals, but many fractions *can* be changed into decimals.

Every fraction represents its numerator divided by its denominator. So $\frac{5}{8} = 5 \div 8$. Set up a division problem. Add a decimal point and as many placeholder zeros as you need in your dividend. As you can see, $\frac{5}{8} = .625$, six hundred twenty-five thousandths.

Example: Change $\frac{5}{8}$ to a decimal.

```
      .625
  8)5.000
    4.8
     20
     16
     40
     40
```

Exercises   CHANGE FRACTIONS TO DECIMALS

Round to the nearest ten-thousandth.

1 $\frac{5}{16}$

2 $\frac{4}{7}$

3 $\frac{15}{31}$

4 $\frac{3}{5}$

5 $\frac{5}{212}$

6 $\frac{31}{33}$

7 $\frac{45}{157}$

8 $\frac{12}{13}$

9 $\frac{1}{2001}$

10 $\frac{23}{76}$

11 $\frac{3}{32}$

12 $\frac{55}{66}$

13 $\frac{12}{47}$

14 $\frac{7}{8}$

15 $\frac{13}{15}$

16 $\frac{13}{17}$

Changing Decimals to Fractions

Can you also change decimals to fractions?
Yes, and it is much easier to do than changing
fractions into decimals.

Begin by looking at the place value farthest to
the right. Use that as your denominator. The
number becomes the numerator. After you
have changed the decimal into a fraction, you
might even be able to reduce it.

Example:

$$.72 = \frac{72}{100} = \frac{18}{25}$$

Exercises   CHANGE DECIMALS TO FRACTIONS

1 .85

2 .77

3 .888

4 .0125

5 .678

6 .6255

7 .331

8 .4545

9 .876

10 .3125

11 .3435

12 .7007

13 .336

14 .2141

15 .56

16 .0055

8.4

Name _____

Comparing and Ordering Decimals

How do you know which decimals are greater or less than others? If you look at place values, it is easy. Just as you can compare and order whole numbers, you can do the same with decimals. Make sure you line up the decimals so that the decimal points are all in the same column. As with whole numbers, each digit is one place value *higher* than the digit to its immediate right.

When comparing numbers with decimals, always look at the whole number parts first. If two whole numbers are the same, *then* compare moving right from the decimal point. To compare decimals like .07 and .072, you can imagine a placeholder zero to make them both fill the same number of places. So .07 = .070. That is less than .072.

Example:
Order these decimals:
5.62, 6.186, 0.2, .07, 5.65, .071, .009

5.62

6.186

0.2

.07

5.65

.071

.009

The order, reading from highest to lowest is:
6.186, 5.65, 5.62, 0.2, .071, .009

Exercises   COMPARE

Each problem will have 3 numbers: a lowest, middle, and largest number. You will be told which of the three to select: lowest, middle or largest.

1 4, 5, and 10   Lowest

_____

2 10.01, 10.10, and 10.11   Middle

_____

3 .567, .5677, and .56   Largest

_____

4 45.45, 45.449, and 45.4449   Middle

_____

5 14.125, 14.0126, and 14.00126   Lowest

_____

6 21.21, 21.211, and 21.2121   Lowest

_____

7 11.1, 11.11, and 11.111   Largest

_____

8 12.12, 12.102, and 12.1023   Middle

_____

9 166.66, 166.60, and 166.6607   Middle

_____

10 144.32, 14.432, and 1.4432   Largest

_____

11 25.025, 25.205, and 25.502   Middle

_____

12 156.12, 157.01, and 158.32   Lowest

_____

Adding Decimals

To add decimals, first line up your addends by place value. Once you do that, adding decimals is *exactly* the same as adding whole numbers.

Example: 79.46 + 8.65

```
  79.46
+  8.65
-------
  88.11
```

Remember...

Put a decimal point in its proper column in the total, too!

Exercises   ADD

1
```
  45.45
+  2.1
```

2
```
  33.7
+ 41.22
```

3
```
   5.4
+  8.54
```

4
```
   2.22
+  3.001
```

5
```
  33.045
+  .011
```

6
```
   9.0901
+ 13.245
```

7
```
   .782
+  5.6
```

8
```
  454.32
+   2.111
```

9
```
   4.5
+  9.5001
```

10
```
  63.1
+  5.46
```

11
```
  2.22201
+    7.38
```

12
```
   8.704
+ 18.0001
```

13
```
  4.147
+ 5.963
```

14
```
   9.46
+ 55.7222
```

15
```
    .00152
+ 152.1522
```

16
```
  3.202
+ 2.3031
```

17
```
  9.781
+ 1.832
```

18
```
  2.2222
+ 8.888
```

19
```
  478.654
+   3.9702
```

20
```
   3.303
+ 19.0771
```

Name _____

Subtracting Decimals

When you subtract decimals, remember to line up the decimal points. Put in placeholder zeros, if you need to.

Example: 243 − 178.961

$$
\begin{array}{r}
243.000 \\
- 178.861 \\
\hline
64.139
\end{array}
$$

Remember...

The value of a number does *not* change if you add a decimal point at the end and then put in placeholder zeros. You can use as many placeholder zeros as you need.

Exercises   SUBTRACT

1
$$
\begin{array}{r}
15.45 \\
- 7.82 \\
\hline
\end{array}
$$

2
$$
\begin{array}{r}
48.001 \\
- 5.62 \\
\hline
\end{array}
$$

3
$$
\begin{array}{r}
88.88 \\
- 2.97 \\
\hline
\end{array}
$$

4
$$
\begin{array}{r}
50.202 \\
- 2.5005 \\
\hline
\end{array}
$$

5
$$
\begin{array}{r}
10.3 \\
- 4.777 \\
\hline
\end{array}
$$

6
$$
\begin{array}{r}
100.111 \\
- 5.374 \\
\hline
\end{array}
$$

7
$$
\begin{array}{r}
565.002 \\
- 12.345 \\
\hline
\end{array}
$$

8
$$
\begin{array}{r}
7.701 \\
- 6.994 \\
\hline
\end{array}
$$

9
$$
\begin{array}{r}
5.5514 \\
- 4.61 \\
\hline
\end{array}
$$

10
$$
\begin{array}{r}
12.157 \\
- 5.2 \\
\hline
\end{array}
$$

11
$$
\begin{array}{r}
89.7 \\
- 63.63 \\
\hline
\end{array}
$$

12
$$
\begin{array}{r}
3.561 \\
- 2.9872 \\
\hline
\end{array}
$$

13
$$
\begin{array}{r}
4789.32 \\
- 555.55 \\
\hline
\end{array}
$$

14
$$
\begin{array}{r}
8.651 \\
- 6.98 \\
\hline
\end{array}
$$

15
$$
\begin{array}{r}
45.87 \\
- 33.999 \\
\hline
\end{array}
$$

16
$$
\begin{array}{r}
963.751 \\
- 8.8 \\
\hline
\end{array}
$$

17
$$
\begin{array}{r}
8.789 \\
- 1.79 \\
\hline
\end{array}
$$

18
$$
\begin{array}{r}
5.2 \\
- 3.571 \\
\hline
\end{array}
$$

19
$$
\begin{array}{r}
6.91 \\
- 2.84 \\
\hline
\end{array}
$$

20
$$
\begin{array}{r}
8.888 \\
- 2.913 \\
\hline
\end{array}
$$

Adding and Subtracting Money

Whenever you calculate amounts of money, you are adding and subtracting decimals. American money uses decimals, because a dollar is divided into 100 hundredths.

A hundredth of a dollar is "a cent." So if you have 21 dollars and 13 cents, you write it as $21.13, a decimal!

Example: $75 − $38.99

$$\begin{array}{r} \$75.00 \\ - 38.99 \\ \hline \$36.01 \end{array}$$

Remember...

You do not need to put a dollar sign next to all of the addends. However, you need to include a dollar sign in front of the total.

Exercises CALCULATE

1
$$\begin{array}{r} \$56 \\ + \ \$32 \\ \hline \end{array}$$

2
$$\begin{array}{r} \$22.71 \\ + \ \$5.20 \\ \hline \end{array}$$

3
$$\begin{array}{r} \$15 \\ - \ \$12.40 \\ \hline \end{array}$$

4
$$\begin{array}{r} \$11.06 \\ + \ \ \$.32 \\ \hline \end{array}$$

5
$$\begin{array}{r} \$10 \\ - \ \$7.21 \\ \hline \end{array}$$

6
$$\begin{array}{r} \$315.32 \\ - \ \$297.61 \\ \hline \end{array}$$

7
$$\begin{array}{r} \$89.45 \\ - \ \$3.50 \\ \hline \end{array}$$

8
$$\begin{array}{r} \$34 \\ - \ \$4.77 \\ \hline \end{array}$$

9
$$\begin{array}{r} \$1000.03 \\ - \ \$88.42 \\ \hline \end{array}$$

10
$$\begin{array}{r} \$45 \\ + \ \$2.30 \\ \hline \end{array}$$

11
$$\begin{array}{r} \$89 \\ - \ \$56.81 \\ \hline \end{array}$$

12
$$\begin{array}{r} \$813 \\ - \ \$7.71 \\ \hline \end{array}$$

13
$$\begin{array}{r} \$5 \\ - \ \$2.93 \\ \hline \end{array}$$

14
$$\begin{array}{r} \$71.45 \\ - \ \$3.56 \\ \hline \end{array}$$

15
$$\begin{array}{r} \$8.55 \\ - \ \$2.61 \\ \hline \end{array}$$

16
$$\begin{array}{r} \$3.21 \\ - \ \ \$2 \\ \hline \end{array}$$

17
$$\begin{array}{r} \$1561 \\ - \ \$87.87 \\ \hline \end{array}$$

18
$$\begin{array}{r} \$1987.23 \\ - \ \$476.30 \\ \hline \end{array}$$

19
$$\begin{array}{r} \$81 \\ - \ \$22.57 \\ \hline \end{array}$$

20
$$\begin{array}{r} \$45.60 \\ - \ \ \ \$7 \\ \hline \end{array}$$

Name _____

Estimating Decimal Sums and Differences

To estimate sums and differences of decimals, you round just as you would with whole numbers. However, you have to decide what rounding place is the best one to use. If you are estimating money, you may want to round to the nearest dollar. Or you may want to round even closer than the nearest dollar. You can round to the nearest half dollar, or .50. Look at the cents part and ask yourself: Is it closest to 0 dollars, to a $\frac{1}{2}$ dollar, or to 1 dollar?

Example: $12.46 + $11.39

Step 1: $12 + $11 = $23

Step 2: $\frac{1}{2}$ a dollar + $\frac{1}{2}$ a dollar = $1

Step 3: $23 + $1 = $24

Notice that you rounded *both* cents parts *upward* to $\frac{1}{2}$ a dollar. By doing this, you know that your estimated total is *higher* than the actual total.

Exercises   ESTIMATE

1. $34.45
    + $22.52

2. $55.11
    + $22.73

3. $76.77
    + $ 2.31

4. $908.03
    − $ 37.56

5. $32.77
    − $21.99

6. $561.22
    − $ 2.10

7. $77.55
    − $55.77

8. $234.55
    − $222.99

9. $45.32
    + $99.01

10. $10.08
    − $ 1.07

11. $12.77
    + $ 2.39

12. $ 14.57
    + $217.66

13. $21.67
    − $18.33

14. $2.33
    − $1.87

15. $444.71
    + $ 67.33

16. $ 232.47
    + $1001.51

17. $ 67.89
    + $253.77

18. $ 7.52
    + $75.20

19. $2303.41
    + $ 223.67

20. $32.56
    − $21.91

Multiplying Decimals

Is multiplying decimals different from multiplying whole numbers? The technique is basically the same, except for *one* thing. You have to know the *total* number of decimal places in the numbers you multiply.

Example: 33.2 × .46

$$
\begin{array}{r}
33.2 \\
\times\ .46 \\
\hline
1992 \\
13280 \\
\hline
15.272
\end{array}
$$

Notice that you do *not* line up the decimal points when multiplying decimals. You just multiply as if there were no decimal points at all. Do not forget to add placeholder zeros if you need any. When you are finished multiplying, count the total number of decimal places in the **factors**, the numbers you have multiplied. Then, starting from the right of your product, count that number of places, and put your decimal point to the *left* of the last place you counted.

Exercises   MULTIPLY

1
$$
\begin{array}{r}
32.5 \\
\times\ \ .5 \\
\end{array}
$$

2
$$
\begin{array}{r}
45.6 \\
\times\ .33 \\
\end{array}
$$

3
$$
\begin{array}{r}
4.52 \\
\times\ 6.31 \\
\end{array}
$$

4
$$
\begin{array}{r}
789.3 \\
\times\ \ 6.8 \\
\end{array}
$$

5
$$
\begin{array}{r}
1.731 \\
\times\ \ .52 \\
\end{array}
$$

6
$$
\begin{array}{r}
10.01 \\
\times\ 1.01 \\
\end{array}
$$

7
$$
\begin{array}{r}
89.89 \\
\times\ 23.23 \\
\end{array}
$$

8
$$
\begin{array}{r}
4.82 \\
\times\ 88.3 \\
\end{array}
$$

9
$$
\begin{array}{r}
.333 \\
\times\ .444 \\
\end{array}
$$

10
$$
\begin{array}{r}
5.5 \\
\times\ 77.76 \\
\end{array}
$$

11
$$
\begin{array}{r}
842.1 \\
\times\ 2.64 \\
\end{array}
$$

12
$$
\begin{array}{r}
63.4 \\
\times\ 36.5 \\
\end{array}
$$

13
$$
\begin{array}{r}
1.111 \\
\times\ 55.67 \\
\end{array}
$$

14
$$
\begin{array}{r}
51.02 \\
\times\ 3.91 \\
\end{array}
$$

15
$$
\begin{array}{r}
.0013 \\
\times\ .0098 \\
\end{array}
$$

16
$$
\begin{array}{r}
8.5 \\
\times\ 2.3 \\
\end{array}
$$

Multiplying Decimals (cont.)

Is there an easier way to multiply decimals? Sometimes there is. Look at this place value chart.

Example:

$3.52 \times 1000 = 3520$ $3.52 \times .01 = .0352$

Thousands Period			Ones Period			?			
Hundreds	Tens	Ones	Hundreds	Tens	Ones	Tenths	Hundredths	Thousandths	Ten-thousandths
5	7	4,	2	3	2.	9	5	1	8

Each column represents a **power of 10**, which is 10 multiplied by itself one or more times. However, all you need to remember is that each place value is 10 times the place value of the number to its right.

If you keep powers of 10 in mind, you can use a trick. When you multiply a number by a power of ten greater than 1, move the decimal point of the number to the *right*, one place for each power of 10. If you need more places, add placeholder zeros.

When you multiply by a power of 10 that is less than 1, move the decimal point of the number to the *left* for each decimal place in the power of 10.

Exercises MULTIPLY

1
```
  4.6731
×      .1
```

2
```
  71.35
×   100
```

3
```
     .58
×   1000
```

4
```
  16.45
×     .1
```

5
```
  10.005
×    .01
```

6
```
  1.112
× 1000
```

7
```
   .593
×    10
```

8
```
   .322
×  .01
```

9
```
  1056.32
×       .1
```

10
```
  28.90
×     1
```

11
```
  1.56
×   .1
```

12
```
     2.1
× 10000
```

13
```
  58.31
×    10
```

14
```
  81.81
×   100
```

15
```
   .973
×    10
```

16
```
   .002
×  .001
```

Multiplying Money

Since money is a decimal, you can multiply it the same way you multiply other decimals. However, you have to remember *two* important things.

First, you *cannot* multiply money by money. You can multiply money only by a whole number, a fraction, or a decimal.

Second, when you multiply money, the product is *also* money. So if your product has more than two decimal places, you have to round to the nearest hundredth, because money is *always* expressed in dollars and cents (hundredths of a dollar).

Example: $7.26 × 3.8

$$
\begin{array}{r}
\$7.26 \\
\times\ 3.8 \\
\hline
5808 \\
21780\ \\
\hline
27588 = \text{about } \$27.59
\end{array}
$$

Exercises MULTIPLY

1
$$
\begin{array}{r}
\$5.65 \\
\times\ \ 3.2 \\
\end{array}
$$

2
$$
\begin{array}{r}
8.4 \\
\times\ \$96.25 \\
\end{array}
$$

3
$$
\begin{array}{r}
34.2 \\
\times\ \$2.25 \\
\end{array}
$$

4
$$
\begin{array}{r}
\$3.01 \\
\times\ \ 5.6 \\
\end{array}
$$

5
$$
\begin{array}{r}
6.3 \\
\times\ \$2.45 \\
\end{array}
$$

6
$$
\begin{array}{r}
\$5.57 \\
\times\ \ .15 \\
\end{array}
$$

7
$$
\begin{array}{r}
64.3 \\
\times\ \$7.88 \\
\end{array}
$$

8
$$
\begin{array}{r}
\$12.33 \\
\times\ 10.35 \\
\end{array}
$$

9
$$
\begin{array}{r}
\$13.50 \\
\times\ \ 85.3 \\
\end{array}
$$

10
$$
\begin{array}{r}
\$5.01 \\
\times\ 96.85 \\
\end{array}
$$

11
$$
\begin{array}{r}
\$45.55 \\
\times\ \ 3.25 \\
\end{array}
$$

12
$$
\begin{array}{r}
\$78.10 \\
\times\ \ \ 2.1 \\
\end{array}
$$

13
$$
\begin{array}{r}
\$89.99 \\
\times\ \ .011 \\
\end{array}
$$

14
$$
\begin{array}{r}
\$56.37 \\
\times\ \ \ 2.7 \\
\end{array}
$$

15
$$
\begin{array}{r}
\$85.14 \\
\times\ \ 6.62 \\
\end{array}
$$

16
$$
\begin{array}{r}
2.3 \\
\times\ \$9.63 \\
\end{array}
$$

10.3

Estimating Decimal Products

Is there an easy way to estimate the products of decimals? If you know how to round, there is! Just round each factor to its highest place value, and then multiply the rounded amounts.

Example: 212.9 × .327
200 × .3 = 60.0

That is a fairly good estimate. You even know something more about how the estimate compares to the *real* product. Did you notice that you rounded both numbers *downward*? This means your estimate is *less* than the actual product.

Exercises   ESTIMATE

1 505.2 × .322

2 10.71 × 2.31

3 55.5 × 21.2

4 35.67 × .437

5 631.23 × 1.61

6 2.87 × 950

7 7.3 × .51

8 111.159 × .23

9 81.453 × 1.8

10 245.459 × .37

11 93.7123 × .54

12 37.25 × 4.12

13 12.67 × .96543

14 1.111 × 4.2519

15 5.51 × .50001

Name _____

Dividing Decimals by Whole Numbers

Adding, subtracting, and multiplying decimals is similar to working with whole numbers. Is that also true for dividing decimals?

When you divide a decimal by a whole number, *only* the dividend has a decimal point. To calculate correctly, you must line up a decimal point in the quotient with the decimal point in the dividend. That is all there is to it!

Example: $92.4 \div 7$

$$
\begin{array}{r}
13.2 \\
7{\overline{\smash{\big)}\,92.4}} \\
\underline{7} \\
22 \\
\underline{21} \\
14 \\
\underline{14}
\end{array}
$$

Exercises DIVIDE

Round to the nearest ten-thousandth.

1 $5{\overline{\smash{\big)}\,45.7}}$

2 $4{\overline{\smash{\big)}\,29.34}}$

3 $11{\overline{\smash{\big)}\,78.9}}$

4 $7{\overline{\smash{\big)}\,41.8}}$

5 $2{\overline{\smash{\big)}\,2.3}}$

6 $3{\overline{\smash{\big)}\,456.2}}$

7 $7{\overline{\smash{\big)}\,33.3}}$

8 $6{\overline{\smash{\big)}\,89.34}}$

9 $14{\overline{\smash{\big)}\,745.2}}$

10 $7{\overline{\smash{\big)}\,41.9}}$

11 $18{\overline{\smash{\big)}\,22.56}}$

12 $8{\overline{\smash{\big)}\,71.45}}$

13 $4{\overline{\smash{\big)}\,963.5}}$

14 $9{\overline{\smash{\big)}\,65.1}}$

15 $50{\overline{\smash{\big)}\,964.5}}$

16 $75{\overline{\smash{\big)}\,715.1}}$

Name _____

Dividing Whole Numbers by Decimals

Is dividing a whole number by a decimal different than dividing a decimal by a whole number? Only a little bit. However, you need to remember one simple trick. You want to move the decimal point of the divisor all the way to the right. So you must multiply the divisor by whatever power of 10 will do that. Then, you have to also multiply the dividend by that same power of 10.

You can put a decimal point at the end of the new dividend and add as many placeholder zeros as you need. If you do that, though, do not forget to put the decimal point in the quotient!

Example: $27 \div .08$

$.08 \times 100 = 8$ $\qquad$ $27 \times 100 = 2700$

$$
\begin{array}{r}
337.5 \\
8{\overline{\smash{)}2700.0}} \\
\underline{24} \\
30 \\
\underline{24} \\
60 \\
\underline{56} \\
40 \\
\underline{40}
\end{array}
$$

Exercises   DIVIDE

Round to the nearest ten-thousandth.

1 $2.4{\overline{\smash{)}5}}$

2 $9.1{\overline{\smash{)}6}}$

3 $6.3{\overline{\smash{)}55}}$

4 $23.1{\overline{\smash{)}654}}$

5 $8.8{\overline{\smash{)}96}}$

6 $4.5{\overline{\smash{)}33}}$

7 $7.1{\overline{\smash{)}41}}$

8 $7.7{\overline{\smash{)}14}}$

9 $8.9{\overline{\smash{)}72}}$

10 $2.5{\overline{\smash{)}439}}$

11 $6.1{\overline{\smash{)}428}}$

12 $6.8{\overline{\smash{)}55}}$

13 $9.8{\overline{\smash{)}54}}$

14 $9.09{\overline{\smash{)}81}}$

15 $3.5{\overline{\smash{)}56}}$

16 $5.5{\overline{\smash{)}89}}$

Dividing Decimals by Decimals

Now you know how to divide a whole number by a decimal and a decimal by a whole number. Can you figure out how to divide a decimal by a decimal?

Example: .429 ÷ .05

.05 × 100 = 5   .429 × 100 = 42.9

```
      8.58
  5)42.90
    40
     29
     25
      40
      40
```

If you said "multiply the divisor and the dividend by the same power of 10," you are correct. First, look at the divisor and find the smallest power of 10 that will move the decimal point all the way to the right. Then multiply both the divisor and the dividend by that power of 10.

Notice in this example that you have to add a placeholder zero to the dividend.

Remember...

You always want the divisor to be a whole number, so you must multiply it by a power of 10. Then, *always* multiply the dividend by the same power of 10.

Exercises **DIVIDE**

Round to the nearest ten-thousandth.

1 4.5)11.2

2 2.5)5.7

3 8.1)88.3

4 2.1)4.5

5 7.88)5.98

6 2.33)17.1

7 2.3)8.56

8 2.222)5.12

9 3.41)4.6

10 2.11)6.54

11 2.37)6.01

12 5.55)6.44

13 3.03)9.1

14 2.1)987.1

15 3.71)8.89

16 2.45)56.98

Name _____

Dividing Money

Dividing money is *exactly* like dividing any other kind of decimal. However, you need to remember the following:

If you are dividing money, money *must* be in your dividend. If your divisor is also money, your quotient will *not* be money. If your divisor is *not* money, your quotient *will* be money.

Remember...

If your quotient is money, you need to round it to the nearest cent (hundredth).

Example 1: How many times does $4 go into $12?

$12 ÷ $4 = 3. Your divisor is money, so your quotient is *not*.

Example 2: How much is $12 ÷ 4?

$12 ÷ 4 = $3. Your divisor is *not* money, so your quotient is.

Exercises   DIVIDE

Round to the nearest cent.

1   $3)$15

2   $5)$56

3   $3.25)$89

4   2.3)$10

5   5.5)$4.25

6   $4.50)$25.25

7   2.1)$78.89

8   $8.25)$42.50

9   5.5)$45.45

10   $2.33)$5.01

11   $6.54)$89.25

12   10.2)$9800.12

13   $5.55)$96.65

14   $6.51)$45.12

15   7.55)$99.50

16   4.1)$8.88

Estimating Decimal Quotients

There are *two* ways to estimate decimal quotients. Can you figure out what they are? In both methods, you need to drop the decimal.

Which way do you think will most often make your estimate closer to the actual quotient? The second way will *usually* get you closer.

Which estimate was better? Do the division problem and find out!

Example 1: Drop the decimals parts in both numbers and round as you would normally, looking for **compatible numbers**.

$$33.06 \div 4.1$$

$$33 \div 4$$

Compatible numbers $= 33 \div 3 = 11$

Example 2: Round **first** and then drop the decimals.

$33.06 \div 3.8$ 33.06 rounds to 33

3.8 rounds to 4 $33 \div 4 = 8.25 = 8$ (rounded)

Exercises   ESTIMATE

Use the estimating method from Example 1 to complete questions 1–8.

1 $313.2 \div 3.322 =$ **2** $10.71 \div 2.31 =$ **3** $33.3 \div 21.2 =$ **4** $33.67 \div .837 =$

5 $631.23 \div 1.61 =$ **6** $2.87 \div 130 =$ **7** $7.3 \div .31 =$ **8** $111.131 \div 5.23 =$

Use the estimating method from Example 2 to complete questions 9–17.

9 $13.7123 \div 4.38 =$ **10** $37.23 \div 8.12 =$ **11** $12.67 \div 1.86383 =$

12 $211.111 \div 8.2311 =$ **13** $43.31 \div 2.30001 =$ **14** $71.36 \div 3.33 =$

15 $66.2882 \div 10.101 =$ **16** $87.23 \div 9.1101 =$ **17** $78.3 \div 4.20101 =$

12.1

Understanding Percent

Percents are special kinds of ratios, expressed as decimals. *Per* means *by*, and *cent* means hundredth. **Percents** compare numbers by looking at a whole as if it were divided into 100 parts.

Example:

60% = .60 = .6

6% = .06

Remember...

Every percentage can be displayed as a decimal or a fraction with a denominator of 100.

Exercises **WRITE DECIMALS AND FRACTIONS**

Convert to a decimal and a fraction.

1 7% = _____ = _____

2 16% = _____ = _____

3 100% = _____ = _____

4 25% = _____ = _____

5 1% = _____ = _____

6 20% = _____ = _____

7 44% = _____ = _____

8 99% = _____ = _____

9 23% = _____ = _____

10 3% = _____ = _____

11 0% = _____ = _____

12 71% = _____ = _____

13 Out of 100 questions on an exam, Geraldine answered 89 questions correctly. What percentage of questions did Geraldine answer correctly?

_____

14 Frederick is dividing his birthday cake among 10 friends. If each person receives an equal 10% of the cake, how can Frederick use fractions to express a single slice of cake?

_____

How can Frederick use decimals to express a single slice of cake?

_____

Percents and Fractions

Can you express percents in ways other than as a decimal?

Example:

What is 30% of 50?

$$\frac{30}{100} \times 50 = \frac{1500}{100} = 15$$

Just as you can with other decimals, you can change percents into fractions. The denominator of a percent is *always* 100, and the numerator will be the number of the percent.

$$\frac{2}{5} = ?\%$$

$$100 \div 5 = 20 \qquad 2 \times 20 = 40$$

$$\frac{2}{5} = 40\%$$

Some fractions can be turned into simple percents. If the denominator of the fraction can divide evenly into 100, find the quotient. Then multiply the numerator by the quotient, and add the percent sign. If the denominator of the fraction cannot divide evenly into 100, the fraction *cannot* be converted into a simple percent.

Remember...

Some fractions cannot be easily changed to percents. If 100 cannot be divided evenly by the fraction's denominator, you will not be able to convert the fraction to a simple percent.

Exercises **CONVERT**

Convert the fractions to a simple percentage, or state that the fraction cannot be converted to a simple percentage.

1. $\frac{1}{2} = $ _____

2. $\frac{3}{20} = $ _____

3. $\frac{7}{15} = $ _____

4. $\frac{3}{10} = $ _____

5. $\frac{2}{3} = $ _____

6. $\frac{3}{4} = $ _____

7. $\frac{6}{11} = $ _____

8. $1 = $ _____

9. $\frac{1}{32} = $ _____

10. $\frac{4}{25} = $ _____

11. $\frac{19}{50} = $ _____

12. $\frac{3}{50} = $ _____

13. $\frac{14}{10} = $ _____

14. $\frac{11}{20} = $ _____

15. $\frac{3}{25} = $ _____

16. $\frac{4}{9} = $ _____

17. $\frac{7}{20} = $ _____

18. $200 = $ _____

Name _____

Percents and Decimals

How can you convert decimals with thousandths, ten-thousandths, and even smaller places into percentages? Simply move the decimal two places to the right and add a percent sign.

Example:

Convert .46072 to a percent.

.46072 = 46.072%

In this example, move the decimal point two places to the right. Then add the percent sign.

Exercises   CONVERT

Convert the decimals to a percentage. If the number is already a percentage, convert it to a decimal.

1 7% = _____

2 18.5% = _____

3 .33 = _____

4 .675 = _____

5 .3356 = _____

6 .01% = _____

7 2.34% = _____

8 3.45 = _____

9 2.145 = _____

10 .3% = _____

11 33.29% = _____

12 2456 = _____

13 Taylor divided 6 shares of XYZ Corporation among 7 of her cousins. Each cousin received .8571 shares of XYZ stock. What percentage of a whole share did each cousin receive?

_____

14 Bill wants to take 15.43% of his earnings this year and put his money in his savings account. If Bill earned $100 this year, how much money will he put into his savings account?

_____

Multiplying Percents and Fractions

Can you multiply percents and fractions? Yes, you can. You learned that percents can be expressed as a fraction. So you need to convert the percent to a fraction and then multiply the two fractions.

An even simpler way to multiply a fraction by a percent is to multiply the percent *as if it were a whole number* times the fraction. The product will almost always be an improper fraction. Change that fraction into a mixed number and add the percent sign.

Example:

What is 50% of $\frac{2}{3}$?

$50\% = \frac{1}{2}$ $\frac{1}{2} \times \frac{2}{3} = \frac{1}{3}$

What is $\frac{1}{6}$ of 96%?

$\frac{1}{6} \times \frac{96}{100} = \frac{96}{600} = \frac{16}{100} = 16\%$

Remember...

Remember these two important points:

If you find a percent of a fraction, the product will be a fraction.

If you multiply a fraction by a percent, the product will be a percent.

Exercises   MULTIPLY

1. $\frac{1}{2}$ of 40% =

2. $\frac{2}{3}$ of 60% =

3. 50% of 18 =

4. 12% of 400 =

5. $\frac{1}{4}$ of 8% =

6. 20% of 75 =

7. 39% of 300 =

8. $\frac{1}{9}$ of 45% =

9. $\frac{1}{3}$ of 90% =

10. 25% of 60 =

11. $\frac{1}{3}$ of 27% =

12. 18% of 50 =

13. 120% of 35 =

14. 100% of 37 =

15. $\frac{1}{4}$ of 36% =

Name _____

Simple Interest

What does *simple interest* mean in a loan or a bank account? How do you calculate simple interest?

The amount you borrowed or deposited into the bank is called the **principal**. Simple interest is a percent of the principal that has to be paid by you if you borrowed the money, or by the bank if you deposited the money. In both cases, the interest is *added* to the principal.

Example:

How much simple interest would you earn on a deposit of $500 that remained in the bank for one year at 4% interest?

Principal = $500

Rate of Interest for one year = 4%

Principal (p) × Rate of Interest (r)

Interest (i) = p × r

$i = \$500$ loan at 4% $= \$500 \times \dfrac{4}{100} = \$20$

Suppose you borrow the same amount of money at the same interest rate. How much would you have to pay back to the bank if the loan was paid in one year? You would have to pay p + i = $500 (the principal) + $20 (the interest) = $520

Exercises   SOLVE

1 If the simple interest earned on $200 is $50, how much would you be earning on $700?

_____

2 A principal of $3000 will earn how much simple interest at 7.2%?

_____

3 Your uncle gives you $100 and deposits it into a savings account that pays simple interest of 6% per year. How much will you earn in interest for the year?

_____

4 At the beginning of the year you have $450 in your savings account and you are earning simple interest of 3.5% for the year. How much will you have at the end of the year?

_____

5 Simple interest at 7% on $5,000 would be how much?

_____

6 Simple interest at 1% is how much for a principal of $10,000?

_____

7 If you have a principal of $4,000 and earn simple interest of 5% for one year, how much will you have at the end of the year?

_____

8 How much will you earn in a year on $150 if the simple interest is paid at a rate of 11%?

_____

Simple Interest for More or Less than One Year

Does simple interest always have to be figured for exactly one year? No, you can calculate simple interest for longer or shorter time periods.

You still multiply the principal by the rate. But you *also* multiply by the number of years. It does not matter if the number of years is greater than, or less than 1!

Example:

Principal (Bank Account) = $250

Rate of Interest for one year: $6\frac{1}{2}\%$

Total number of years = 4

Interest = Principal (p) × Interest Rate (r) × Years (y)

Interest = $250 x .065 x 4 = $65

Principal (Bank Account) = $300

Rate of Interest for one year: 5%

Total number of years = $\frac{3}{4}$

Interest = Principal (p) × Interest Rate (r) × Years (y)

Interest = $300 × .05 × $\frac{3}{4}$ = $11.25

Exercises   SOLVE

Round all answers to the nearest cent.

1 How much simple interest would you earn if you had $10,000 and you were being paid 5% for 15 months?

_____

2 If you invest $5,600 for 18 months at a simple interest rate of 7%, how much would you earn?

_____

3 What would be the total amount that you would have after 7 months if you started with $2,700 and were paid simple interest of 5.5%?

_____

4 If you start with $6,275 and earn simple interest of 14.75% for 37 months, what would be your total earnings for the period?

_____

5 You have a principal of $45,200 and will receive simple interest of 19.5% for 4 years. How much interest will you earn?

_____

6 What would be the simple interest earned on $2,350 at 9.27% for 23 months?

_____

Unit Test

Lessons 8–12

Round to the nearest tenth.

1 3406.997 _____

2 334,782.099 _____

3 65,529.0887 _____

4 12.94996 _____

Round to the nearest hundredth.

5 2,467,891.3554 _____

6 12.4532 _____

7 97.009 _____

8 17.61093 _____

Round to the nearest ten thousandth.

9 467,001.35545 _____

10 199.11115 _____

11 1,683,679.57344 _____

12 8.194301 _____

Convert decimals to fractions.

13 .8 _____

14 .875 _____

15 .08 _____

16 .625 _____

Convert fractions to decimals.

17 $\dfrac{3}{5}$ _____

18 $\dfrac{8}{15}$ _____

19 $\dfrac{3}{16}$ _____

20 $6\dfrac{1}{8}$ _____

Put the decimals in order from greatest to least.

21 .122, .1145, .616, .6165, .513, .3132, .2126, .819

_____

22 .217, .0217, .0133, .0487, .1243, .20413, .5257, .05257, .05205

_____

Unit Test

Lessons 8–12

Add or subtract.

23 1.157397
  + 2.31542

24 3.10341056
  + 3.431776

25 1.1564
   2.1667
  + 3.337833

26 4.15466
  − 2.2355

27 1.892754
  − .464043

28 2.4276
  − .17813344

29 $1.25
  + $5.5

30 $1.89
  + $ .89

Multiply or divide.

31 .4033
  ×   90

32 14.615
  × 145

33 25)$2.67

34 4.539
  × 1.65

35 $ .56
  × 1.64

36 1.7965
  × 1.657

37 $1.25
  +   5.5

38 24)35.487

39 2.24)14.293415

40 .23)$2.69

41 .025).5805

42 18)25.5418

Estimate, then multiply or divide.

43 .3134572
  ×   .34

44 .225).143143

45 1214
  × .25

46 .40)5502

47 60.50
  × 1.5

48 5.5)250.90

49 81.81
  × 3.765

50 .333)18.4545

Name _____

Lessons 8–12

Calculate.

51 30% of $1\dfrac{2}{5}$

52 40% of 440

53 $\dfrac{1}{4}$ of 48%

54 $\dfrac{2}{5}$ of 70%

55 $\dfrac{3}{8}$ of 340%

56 43% of .705

57 84% of 1.906

58 75% of .7575

59 Flora went to the stationery store to buy tools for her art class.
She spent $2.50 on colored pencils, $7.05 on a set of artist pallets,
$4.59 for a used straight edge, $2.09 for a lined memo pad, and $5.28
for a new water bottle. How much did she spend altogether? _____

If Flora only brought thirty dollars with her,
did she have enough money? _____

If so, how much change should she get back? _____

If not, how much more money does she need? _____

60 Thad and his chess club raised a total of $563.75 for the local homeless
shelter. There are 11 people in the chess club. If each member raised
the same amount of money, how much did each member raise? _____

61 Jane went to the store to buy food for a party of 8 friends. She spent $3.75
on each person for soup, $1.15 each for a warm beverage, and $.76 each
for a piece of fruit. How much did she spend in total to buy the food? _____

She brought two twenty dollar bills with her. Did she have enough money? _____

62 Jessie deposited $824.25 of his babysitting money into
an account that pays 4.5% interest. How much will he
have in his account at the end of one year? _____

63 What is the annual rate of interest on a loan of $1,500 if
you have paid a total of $120 in interest after two years? _____

64 Chris borrowed $200 from his brother and told him he
would pay the money back with interest. If the interest rate is 12%,
what is the total that Chris will owe his brother after 6 months? _____

If Chris waits a full year to pay his brother, how much will
he owe him, in total? _____

Bar Graphs

In order to remember facts, some people need to be able to visualize them. Is there some way you can picture numerical information?

A **Bar Graph** uses bars to display **data**, or information, comparing two or more people, places, or things. The bars can be compared to one another because each one represents a number.

For example, there are 50 students in the 7th grade at Thomas Jefferson Middle School. Each student voted for a favorite vegetable. The vertical axis shows the number of students, and the horizontal axis show the various vegetables.

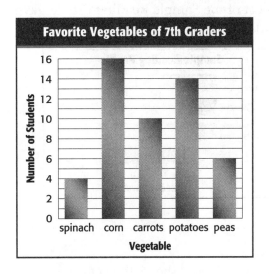

Exercises **INTERPRET**

1 Your neighborhood diner is preparing breakfast for 100 hungry customers. Using the information in the chart below, what type of eggs should the cook prepare the least of?

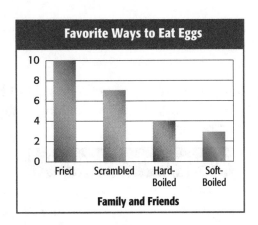

2 You are responsible for ordering food for all of the animals at the shelter. Using this chart, which two groups of animals would you order the least amount of food for?

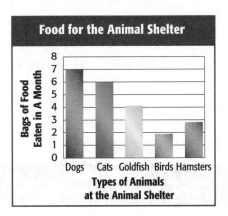

3 According to the chart below, which aspect of the Sample Reading Profile gave students the most difficulty?

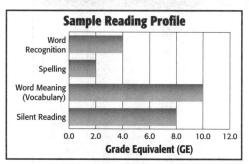

_____

4 According to the chart below, what student won the ice cream eating contest?

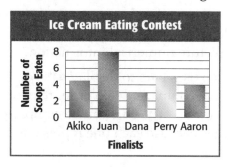

_____

5 The chart below shows the years of teaching experience for Pleasant Hill High School. Where do the majority of teachers fall?

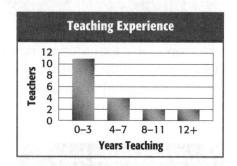

_____

6 What two letter grades in the chart below had the lowest percentages of students receiving that grade?

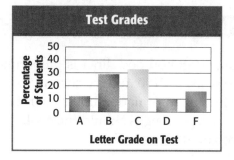

_____

7 What conclusion can you make about student performance at Fitchburg State College from the chart below?

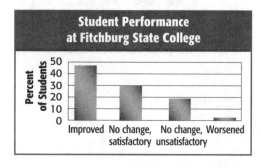

_____

_____

8 Can you make any conclusions about the trend of temperatures by looking at the chart below?

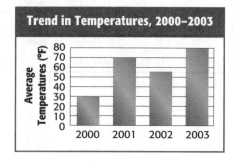

_____

_____

Line Graphs

Can you show data for something that changes as time passes? You might use a **Line Graph**, which shows how information changes over time.

The numbers on the horizontal axis are dates. The distance from one date to another is shown in **intervals** of 5 days. When the line segment connecting intervals is steep, there is a great deal of change. A less steep line segment shows less change during that interval.

Looking at this graph, in what time periods did Mr. Jones do the most driving? The least driving?

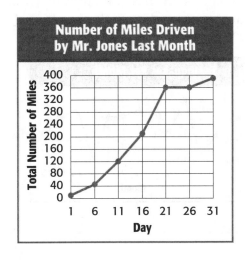

Number of Miles Driven by Mr. Jones Last Month

---

1 The guide at the Abracadabra Falls Visitor Center tells you that their tourist season lasts all year, not just in the winter or summer. Does the graph shown support this? Why or why not?

_____

_____

_____

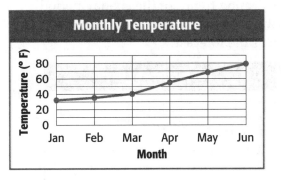

Number of Visitors by Month

2 The Northern Hemisphere experiences winter from December until March. During these months, the Southern Hemisphere is experiencing summer. Looking at the graph shown, is the area represented located in the Northern Hemisphere or Southern Hemisphere?

_____

_____

_____

Monthly Temperature

13.2

Name _____

3 If you are planning a family vacation, what would be the best 2 months to avoid earthquakes, according to the graph below?

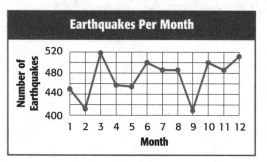

_____

4 Would the graph below support the claim that New Zealand had cut down on its overall greenhouse emissions during the period of 1990 to 2004?

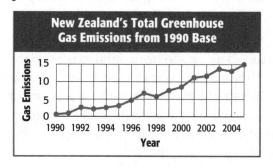

_____

5 Look at the population graph below. Which years represent a steep interval?

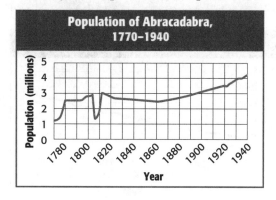

_____

6 Approximately how many people lived in the Southern Region of the U.S. in 1966, according to the line graph below?

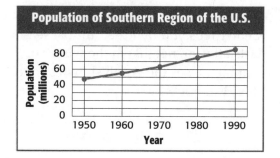

_____

7 The weather reporter forecasted a warming trend for the six-day period shown in the graph below. How accurate was the forecast?

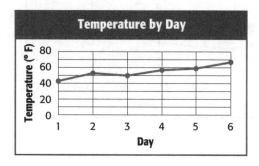

_____

8 The red line in the graph below shows the price of a stock during the period of April to December. What was the approximate high price during the period of April to November?

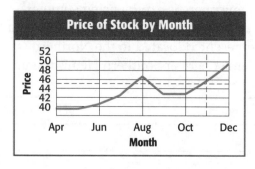

_____

Double-Line Graphs

Is there a way to show how information changes over time for *two or more* people, places, or things? Yes, you could show this information in a **Double-Line Graph**, which compares data for two or more people, places, or things as time passes.

With this graph, you can compare the distances driven by both Mr. and Mrs. Jones at different times during the month.

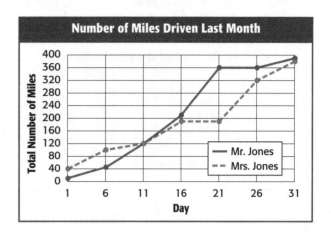

Exercises   INTERPRET

1 What sort of relationship can you see in the graph below between sales and profits?

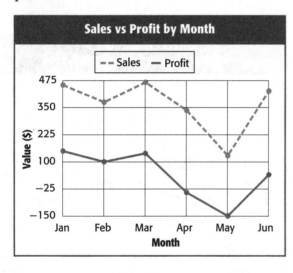

_____

_____

_____

_____

_____

_____

2 There is an old saying that "money does not buy happiness." Does the double-line graph below support that? Why or why not?

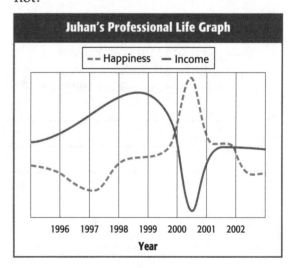

_____

_____

_____

_____

_____

_____

3 In this double-line graph, the life expectancy of males and females appears to stay at a constant difference of about 4 years. What is the good news for males in spite of this? Explain your answer.

_____

_____

_____

_____

_____

_____

Life Expectancy at Birth

Years — y-axis: 70, 72, 74, 76, 78, 80, 82, 84, 86

x-axis: 1981 86 91 96 01 06 11 16 21 26 31 36 41

- - - Females
—— Males

4 Utilizing this triple-line graph. what conclusion can you reach about expenditures for the Criminal Justice system during the period 1982–2006?

_____

_____

_____

_____

_____

_____

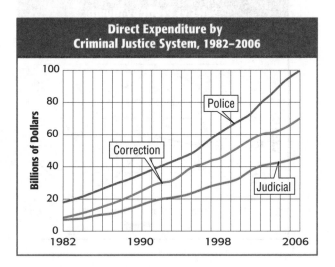

Direct Expenditure by Criminal Justice System, 1982–2006

Billions of Dollars — y-axis: 0, 20, 40, 60, 80, 100

x-axis: 1982, 1990, 1998, 2006

Police
Correction
Judicial

Circle Graphs

Is there a way to compare parts to a whole using a graph? Yes, a **Circle Graph**, or **pie chart**, compares parts to a whole. However, it does not necessarily compare in hundredths, it compares amounts visually, like slices of a pie. *Sometimes*, you can calculate how big a part is exactly, but not always.

The whole circle graph shows the total number of shows that LaWanda watches on TV. It does not *really* show the total number of shows, because the graph compares the types of shows she watches without using numbers. However, if you know that LaWanda regularly spends 16 hours watching TV each week, you *can* calculate some information.

Types of TV Shows LaWanda Watches

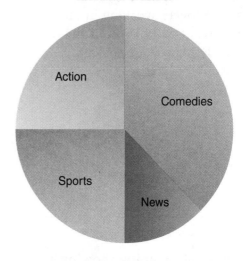

Exercises INTERPRET

1 Does the circle graph below support the idea that a large percentage of money spent on education is applied to non-instructional purposes? Explain your answer.

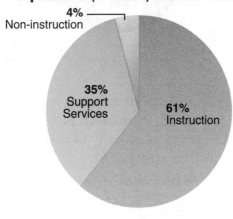

The Cost of an Education: Breakdown of Average Cost per Student Expenditures (in Dollars) for Public Education

_____

_____

_____

_____

2 The graph below represents the distribution of colors in a bag of candies. Should Patrick expect to pick an orange piece of candy if he only gets one pick? Explain your answer.

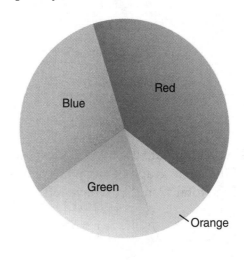

_____

_____

_____

_____

3 The circle graph below shows sales for the prior year at a popular shoe store in Dallas. According to the chart, during what month would the manager need the most employees working in the store? During what month would she need the fewest? Explain your answer.

Sales

_____

4 The circle graph below represents Maria's favorite types of movies. What 2 genres, when added together, make up half of the movies Maria watches?

Favorite Type of Movie

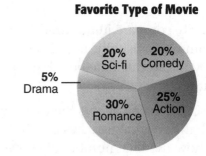

_____

5 Below is a circle graph showing a breakdown of some of the common toppings on a pizza. The crust and the cheese make up what percent of the pizza? How did you reach this answer?

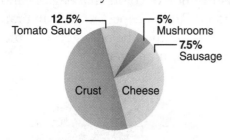

_____

6 Below is a graph showing the costs for a manufacturer in New York City. Does it make sense that she wants to cut over 20% of her costs by focusing largely on reducing the budget for tools? Explain your answer.

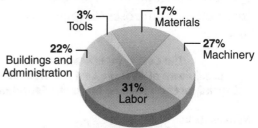

_____

7 If you eliminate the two smallest sections of the circle graph below what percentage of the total would you have left?

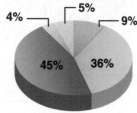

_____

8 According to the information in the circle graph below, is there one type of pie that is preferred by a majority of people? Explain your answer.

Pie Preferences

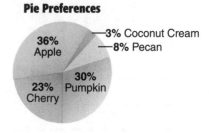

_____

Measures of Central Tendency

What other kinds of comparisons can you make with numbers? You can compare numbers to other numbers using **statistics**, the branch of mathematics that studies data expressed in numbers. Using statistics, you can answer some common questions like: How big, how long, how many, how far, and so on.

There are a number of things you can say about any collection of numbers. The greatest number minus the smallest number is called the **range**. The number that appears most *often* in the collection is called the **mode**. The number that is right in the middle is the **median**. If your collection has an even number of addends, you find the median by adding the two numbers in

the middle and dividing by 2. The total of the whole collection divided by the number of addends is called the **mean**, or the **average**. The range, the mode, the median, and the mean may all be different. Or two or more of them may be the same.

Example: 39, 15, 11, 13, 25, 30, 43, 13, 18

Step 1: Order 11, 13, 13, 15, 18, 25, 30, 39, 43

Range = 43 − 11 = 32

Mode = 13   Median = 18

Mean = 11 + 13 + 13 + 15 + 18
       + 25 + 30 + 39 + 43) ÷ 9
       = 207 ÷ 9 = 23

Exercises   CALCULATE

1 Calculate the mean of
[3.2, 2.5, 2.1, 3.7, 2.8, 2.0]

_____

2 Find the median of
[7, 4, 5, 5, 6, 8, 2]

_____

3 Calculate the range of
[43, −22, 5, 10, 31, 4]

_____

4 Find the mode of
[2, 3, 5, 6, 4, 3, 3, 1]

_____

5 Find the mode of
[7, 4, 5, 5, 6, 8, 2]

_____

6 Calculate the range of
[1, −1, 0, 2, −2, −7]

_____

7 Calculate the mean of
[10, 11, −9, 14, 22, 61, −2]

_____

8 Find the median of
[4, 12, 7, 5, 9, 22, 23, 19, 21]

_____

9 Calculate the mean of
[−22, −21, 44, 37, 100, 2.75]

_____

10 Find the mode of
[13, 12, 14, 15, 13, 12, 12, 11, 13, 15, 16]

_____

14.2

Stem-and-Leaf Plots

Can you use charts to show statistics? Yes, there are many ways to show statistics in charts. For example, a **Stem-and-Leaf Plot** organizes data by the place-value of digits. It is named because it reminded some people of a plant with stems, each of which had a different number of leaves.

Example:

Data = 93, 62, 75, 88, 93, 91, 72, 61, 86, 79, 93, 75, 68, 77

Stems	Leaves
6	1 2 8
7	2 5 5 7 9
8	8 6
9	1 3 3 3

Each leaf is attached to the stem to its left. Therefore, the top line represents the numbers 61, 62, and 68. If a number is repeated in the data, you must include *each* repeat in your plot.

Exercises INTERPRET

1 What is the range of the numbers represented in the stem-and-leaf plot below?

_____

Stem	Leaf
9	0 6
8	3 5 7
7	1 6 6 7 8
6	0 2 2 4 4 5 6 8 8
5	1 1 2 2 4 5 7
4	3 4 7 8
3	5 7
2	
1	6

2 Generate the number set represented by the stem-and-leaf plot below.

_____

Stem	Leaf
1	0 7 9
2	1 1 3 4 6 7 8
3	0 1 3 5 6 7 7
4	0 1 1 1 2
5	
6	9

3 Generate the number set represented by the stem-and-leaf plot below.

_____

Stem	Leaf
8	0 5
7	1 5 6
6	
5	1 6 8
4	0 6

4 What is the range of the numbers represented by the stem-and-leaf plot below?

_____

Stem	Leaf
2	2 6 7
3	1 3 5
4	2 4 6
5	7 8 9
6	1 3 4 5 7

Name _____

Box-and-Whisker Plots

You may have heard of a **Box-and-Whisker Plot**, which allows you to quickly look at data to tell where most of the numbers lie.

Example

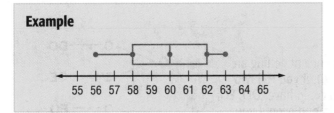

The lowest number in your set of data is called the **lower extreme**. The greatest number is called the **upper extreme**. The median of all the data, as you have learned, is the number in the exact middle of the collection. The median of the numbers from the lower extreme to the median is called the **lower quartile**. The median of the numbers from the median to the upper extreme is called the **upper quartile**.

The word "quartile" is related to "quarter," or fourth. Each outer section of the plot, from the extreme to the nearest quartile, contains one quarter of the data. The box in the middle, extending from the lower quartile to the upper quartile, contains two quarters—or *half*—of the data.

Exercises INTERPRET

1 Which of the three classes has the widest range of scores? The smallest range?

Widest Range _____

Smallest Range _____

2 Which class has the highest median score?

_____

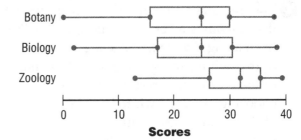

Make a box-and-whisker plot with the following data:

Minimum – 15
Q1 – 25
Q2 – 35
Q3 – 45
Maximum 55

3 What is the range of this plot? The median?

Range _____

Median _____

4 What is the lower quartile? The upper quartile?

Lower Quartile _____

Upper Quartile _____

Name _____

Tree Diagrams

Are there other mathematical visual aids named after things we might see every day? Yes, there is a **Tree Diagram**, which looks like a tree with branches. A tree diagram can be used to show possible combinations of people, places, or things.

Example:

If you roll a six-sided number cube you have an equal chance of getting an odd number (O = 1, 3, 5) or an even number (E = 2, 4, 6). If you roll two number cubes, there are four different combinations you could have: OO; EO; OE; EE. How many possible combinations are there of odd and even if you roll three number cubes?

Count the number of branches on the right of the diagram to find out how many possible combinations there are.

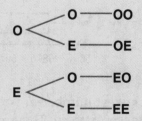

Exercises   INTERPRET AND CREATE

1 The tree diagram at the right illustrates the outcomes when you choose two balls from a bag that contains a large number of red, white, and green balls. How many of these outcomes result in you not choosing at least 1 white ball? How many of these outcomes result in you choosing both a red and a green ball?

_____

_____

_____

First Stage	Second Stage	Outcome
red		RR
		RW
		RG
white		WR
		WW
		WG
green		GR
		GW
		GG

2 Draw a tree diagram to describe the following situation: You go to the ice cream store and you have a choice of vanilla, chocolate, or strawberry ice cream. On your ice cream, you can get either nuts or sprinkles.

Venn Diagrams

What other kinds of diagrams can be used to show data? Have you seen a **Venn Diagram**? A Venn Diagram is used to show groups of data when some data can be placed in *more than one group*.

Example:

Animals Larger than People

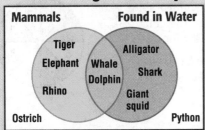

This Venn Diagram shows two groupings for animals that are larger than people. A few large animals can be placed in both groups, while some large animals cannot be placed in either group. What animals are placed in both groups?

Exercises **DIAGRAM**

1. This Venn Diagram represents numbers that are even and numbers that are divisible by the variable *b*. What does their intersection represent?

_____

_____

_____

_____

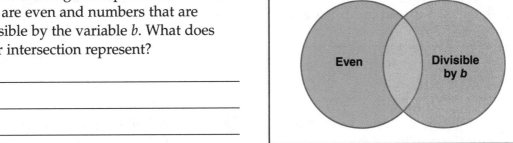

2. Make a Venn Diagram of people who are kickball fans, and people who are baseball fans. The only person that is a fan of both is your friend Kelsey.

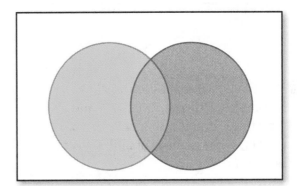

Calculating Probabilities

Imagine that you want to play a game with a spinner that has the numbers from 1 to 8. You need a 6 or higher to win. Can you figure out how likely you are to spin a good number?

Yes, you can calculate the **probability**, or the likelihood of something occurring. When you figure probability, you are making a prediction using mathematics. Calculating probability will tell you what will *probably* happen, but it cannot tell you what will *definitely* happen.

There is a formula to figure out probability (P). It is the number of favorable outcomes (f) divided by the total number of *all* possible outcomes (o). In mathematical terms: $P = \frac{f}{o}$.

Example:

There are 3 favorable outcomes. You could spin a 6, a 7, or an 8.

There are 8 possible numbers to spin.

So $P = \frac{3}{8}$

Exercises   **CALCULATE**

1 If there are 4 girls and 8 boys in a gym class, what is the probability of picking a girl as the person to lead the exercises?

_____

2 In a deck of 52 cards, what is the probability of drawing a king from the deck?

_____

3 There are 4 pizzas: 2 cheese, 1 vegetable and 1 everything. What is the probability that if you open a box, that it will be a cheese pizza?

_____

4 George is 1 of 5 white horses that is in a group of 15 horses in total. If you see a white horse, what is the probability that it is George?

_____

5 You have change in your pocket: 5 quarters, 3 dimes, 2 nickels, and 4 pennies. If you pull a coin out of your pocket, what is the probability that it will be a dime?

_____

6 There are 3 different prizes at the fair: 1 first prize of $100, 3 second prizes of $50 and 5 third prizes of $10. If there are 35 participants in the contest, what is the probability that you will win a prize?

_____

Lessons 13–14

Review the graph and answer the following questions.

1 Is there more trash on the beach due to plastic or paper? _____

2 Which material accounts for more than twice as much trash on the beach as Styrofoam? _____

3 What material accounts for the least amount of trash on the beach? _____

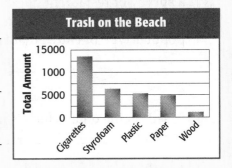

Trash on the Beach

Use data from the graphs to answer the following questions.

4 Which city has the highest average temperature in the summer? _____

The lowest? _____

5 The average temperature of Chicago is 4 degrees warmer than Cleveland, true or false? _____

6 Which city is cooler during the summertime, San Francisco or Milwaukee? _____

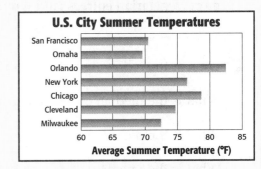

U.S. City Summer Temperatures

7 On what day did Jason practice his guitar the most? _____

The least? _____

8 Jason practices 2.5 hours more on Thursday than on what other day? _____

9 What is the total number of hours that Jason practices from Monday to Saturday? _____

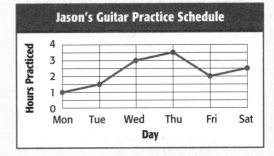

Jason's Guitar Practice Schedule

10 In what year did Rocco hit more home runs than doubles? _____

11 One year, Rocco injured his leg sliding into second base and missed some games while he recovered. What year do you think that was?

_____

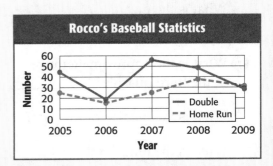

Rocco's Baseball Statistics

Lessons 13–14

12 Fredo is planning the menu for his restaurant. He conducted a survey of restaurant guests and converted that information into a circle graph. Based on the data, what is the most popular type of entree that Fredo's restaurant serves?

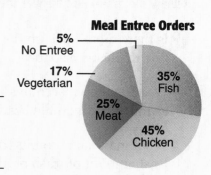

Meal Entree Orders

5% No Entree
17% Vegetarian
35% Fish
25% Meat
45% Chicken

_____

13 Based on the data, which is more popular as an entree, fish or meat? _____

14 Fredo would like to add more vegetarian entrees, but he won't until at least 10% of the patrons want them. Should Fredo add more vegetarian entrees, and why? _____

_____

15 Look at the following data group: 2, 3, 5, 8, 8, 9, 16, 24, 28, 40, 44

What is the median of the data group? _____

What is the mean? _____

What is the range? _____

16 Put the following data into a stem-and-leaf plot:
19, 22, 22, 25, 26, 27, 28, 30, 34, 36, 37, 44, 44, 44, 45, 48, 48, 49, 50, 53, 55, 57, 58, 64, 67

What is the mode of the set of data? _____

What is the median? _____

What is the mean? _____

17 What is the approximate range of the third quartile? _____

What is the median of the data? _____

What is the range of the data? _____

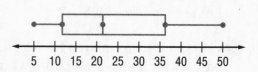

5 10 15 20 25 30 35 40 45 50

Lessons 13–14

18 How many of the outcomes in this tree diagram result in having less than two tails?

_____

First Coin | Second Coin | Third Coin | Outcomes

H — H — H — HHH
H — H — T — HHT
H — T — H — HTH
H — T — T — HTT
T — H — H — THH
T — H — T — THT
T — T — H — TTH
T — T — T — TTT

19 James conducted a survey of students in his class. He found that out of the 50 people he surveyed, 35 used a backpack to carry their books and 28 carried calculators. If 13 students carried a calculator and a backpack, how many students carry only a backpack?

_____

Fill in the Venn Diagram to model the problem.

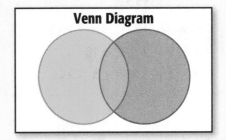

Venn Diagram

20 What does this Venn Diagram tell you?

_____

_____

_____

_____

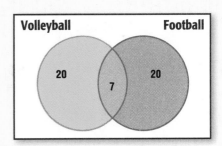

Volleyball   Football

20   7   20

21 You have a bag of 20 markers, 5 of which are green, 3 of which are red, 7 of which are yellow, 3 of which are blue, and 2 of which are orange. What is the chance of reaching into the bag and pulling out a yellow marker?

_____

Anything but a green marker? _____

Name _____

Exponents

What if you want to multiply $3 \times 3 \times 3$? Or $5 \times 5 \times 5 \times 5$? Is there a simple way you can write that? Yes, you can use an **exponent**. The number you keep multiplying by itself is called the **base**. The exponent (written as a small number next to and slightly above the base) tells how many times you multiply the base by itself.

You have already learned about **powers of 10**. Exponents represent powers. So 10^3 is 10 to the third power. Any number can be a base. For example, 3^5 is 3 to the fifth power. When a base is raised to the second power, we use the word "squared." 25^2 can be expressed as "25 to the second power," or "25 squared." When a base is raised to the third power, we often use the word "cubed." So 12^3 can be expressed as "12 cubed."

Here are two important things to know about exponents:

1. A base raised to the **first power** = the base. For example: $197^1 = 197$

2. A base raised to the **zero power** = 1. For example: $9{,}592^0 = 1$

Examples:

$$\text{base} \rightarrow 2^{4 \, \leftarrow \, \text{exponent}} \qquad \text{base} \rightarrow 3^{5 \, \leftarrow \, \text{exponent}}$$

$2^4 = 2 \times 2 \times 2 \times 2 = 16$

$3^5 = 3 \times 3 \times 3 \times 3 \times 3 = 243$

Exercises   CALCULATE

1 $12^2 =$ _____

2 $10^4 =$ _____

3 $7^3 =$ _____

4 $2^3 =$ _____

5 $4^4 =$ _____

6 $5^3 =$ _____

7 $41^2 =$ _____

8 $5^5 =$ _____

9 $6^7 =$ _____

10 $17^4 =$ _____

11 $0^{10} =$ _____

12 $101^0 =$ _____

13 $12^1 =$ _____

14 $24^0 =$ _____

15 $33^1 =$ _____

Exponents (cont.)

Is there a simple way to multiply and divide bases that have exponents? Yes. To multiply a base raised to a power by the same base raised to a power, simply add the exponents. To divide a base raised to a power by the same base raised to a power, simply subtract the exponents.

Examples:

Multiply	Divide
$3^2 \times 3^3 = 3^5$	$4^6 \div 4^4 = 4^2$
$2^4 \times 2^5 = 2^9$	$10^7 \div 10^3 = 10^4$

Exponents can be **negative**. A negative exponent creates a fraction. The numerator is 1. The denominator is the base raised to the power after the minus sign.

Can you multiply and divide a base raised to a negative power by the *same* base raised to a negative power? Yes, you can add and subtract negative exponents, just as you added and subtracted positive exponents. Ignore the negative sign while you add and subtract, but then make sure to include it in your answer.

Example:

For example: $6^{-2} = \dfrac{1}{6^2} = \dfrac{1}{6 \times 6} = \dfrac{1}{36}$

$2^{-6} = \dfrac{1}{2^6} = \dfrac{1}{2 \times 2 \times 2 \times 2 \times 2 \times 2} = \dfrac{1}{64}$

Exercises   MULTIPLY OR DIVIDE

1 $2^3 \div 2^{-5} =$ _____

2 $5^5 \times 5^{-6} =$ _____

3 $11^{11} \div 11^4 =$ _____

4 $54^4 \div 54^{-2} =$ _____

5 $3^2 \div 3^0 =$ _____

6 $8^1 \times 8^8 =$ _____

7 $15^5 \div 15^4 =$ _____

8 $8^6 \div 8^2 =$ _____

9 $18^7 \times 18^{21} =$ _____

10 $81^{10} \div 81^7 =$ _____

11 $19^{19} \times 19^{16} =$ _____

12 $21^2 \div 21^3 =$ _____

13 $15^{-5} \div 15^6 =$ _____

14 $10^{-8} \div 10^{-12} =$ _____

15 $17^{15} \div 17^{22} =$ _____

Scientific Notation

It is difficult to write and read long numbers like 4,500,000,000 or 61,020,000. Is there a simpler way to express long numbers? Yes, you could use **scientific notation**. When you use scientific notation, notice that the decimal is always *greater than 1* but *less than 10*. You might think the difficult part is figuring out which power of 10 to use. However, that is not so hard. Look at the number in standard, or regular, notation. Imagine that there is a

decimal point to the right of that number. Move the decimal point to the left, one place value at a time, counting each time you move it. *Stop* when your number is greater than 1 but less than 10. Your count is the power of 10.

Examples:

$4,500,000,000 = 4.5 \times 10^9$

$61,020,000 = 6.102 \times 10^7$

Exercises   CONVERT

If the expression is in scientific notation, convert it to a number. If it is a number, convert it to scientific notation. Round all numbers to 6 places to the right of the decimal point when converting to scientific notation.

1 $5 \times 10^5 =$

2 $478.23 =$

3 $89,786 =$

4 $6.721 \times 10^6 =$

5 $2.9731 \times 10^{-2} =$

6 $691,273 =$

7 $5.9178 \times 10^{-3} =$

8 $8.72345 \times 10^{10} =$

9 $6,664,475 =$

10 $.0005123 =$

11 $8.9 =$

12 $100.235 =$

13 $963,764 =$

14 $4.6554 =$

15 $789.23 =$

16 $15,896,000,000,000 =$

17 $8,999,345,000 =$

18 $1.697324 \times 10^4 =$

Order of Operations

What happens if you see a long string of mathematical calculations to perform? Is there some way to know where to begin? Yes, you can use a rule called **order of operations**. It tells you in what order you should do calculations in a long string.

There is even a simple word that can help you remember the order of operations: **PEMDAS**. That stands for **P**arentheses, **E**xponents, **M**ultiplication and **D**ivision, **A**ddition and **S**ubtraction.

Example:

Solve: $20 - 5 \times 2 + 36 \div 3^2 - (9 - 2) = ?$

You can solve this problem using order of operations. Remember PEMDAS.

Step 1: Parentheses
$(9 - 2) = 7$
$20 - 5 \times 2 + 36 \div 3^2 - 7 = ?$

Step 2: Exponents
$3^2 = 9$
$20 - 5 \times 2 + 36 \div 9 - 7 = ?$

Step 3: Multiplication and Division
$5 \times 2 = 10$
$36 \div 9 = 4$
$20 - 10 + 4 - 7 = ?$

Step 4: Addition and Subtraction
$20 - 10 = 10$
$10 + 4 = 14$
$14 - 7 = 7$

Exercises   CALCULATE

1 $(4 + 2) \times (4 - 2) - (2 \times 3) + 2^{4-2} =$

2 $(5 - 4) \times (10 - 6) - 2^2 + 4 =$

3 $(4 - 2)^3 + (4 - 2)^2 + 1 - 2 + 2^2 =$

4 $(4 + 2) \times (9 - 7) + 3^2 - (8 - 5)^2 =$

5 $(6 - 4)^3 - (6 - 4)^3 + 2 - (2 - 1) =$

6 $2^2 - (2^3 - 2) + (2^2 + 4) =$

7 $(5 - 2) + (6 - 4) - (3 - 1) =$

8 $(4 + 3) \times (5 - 2) \times (2 - 1)^2 =$

9 $(4 - 2) + (5 \times 2)^2 - 2 \times 12 - 4^2 =$

10 $(1 + 1 + 2) \times 7 - 4^2 =$

11 $(13 - 2) - 3^2 + 10 - (2 \times 4) =$

12 $7^2 + (4 - 1) \times 5 - 2 \times (3 - 1)^3 =$

Name _Rushie_   6-9-5

Commutative and Associative Properties

Are there other rules to use that make math easier? Yes, you can learn the ways numbers behave, or the **properties** of numbers.

Commutative Property of Addition
You can add addends *in any order* without changing the sum.
$7 + 3 + 6 = 6 + 3 + 7$

Commutative Property of Multiplication
You can multiply factors *in any order* without changing the product.
$5 \times 2 \times 9 = 9 \times 5 \times 2$

Associative Property of Addition
You can group addends any way you like without changing the sum.
$(7 + 8) + 3 = 7 + (8 + 3)$

Associative Property of Multiplication
You can group factors any way you like without changing the product.
$(3 \times 12) \times 4 = 3 \times (12 \times 4)$

Exercises   IDENTIFY THE PROPERTY

1 $7 \times 4 \times 3 = 4 \times 3 \times 7$
Commutative property of Multi---

2 $2 + 9 + 22 = 22 + 9 + 2$
Commutative Property of add

3 $3 \times 4 \times 4 \times 2 = 3 \times (4 \times 4) \times 2$
Associative property of Multi---

4 $4 \times 2 \times 3 \times 4 = 2 \times 3 \times 4 \times 4$
Commutative property of Multi---

5 $9 \times 2 \times 4 = 2 \times 4 \times 9$
Commutative Property of Multi--

6 $9 \times 7 \times 9 \times 9 = (9 \times 7) \times (9 \times 9)$
Associative property of Multi

7 $9 + 7 + 1 = 7 + 9 + 1$
Commutative Property of Add

8 $4 \times 11 \times 9 \times 4 = 4 \times 4 \times 9 \times 11$
Commutative property of Multi---

9 $2 + 8 + 6 + 4 = (2 + 8) + (6 + 4)$
Associative property of add

10 $6 \times 4 \times 2 = 4 \times 2 \times 6$
Commutative property of Multi

11 $22 + 21 + 24 + 22 = 22 + (21 + 24) + 22$
Associative property of Add

12 $6 \times 8 + 6 \times 0 = 8 \times 6 + 0 \times 6$
Commutative Property of Multi

The Distributive and Identity Properties

Do numbers have other properties, too? Yes!

The Distributive Property of Multiplication

To multiply a sum of two or more numbers, you can multiply by each number separately, and then *add* the products. To multiply the difference of two numbers, multiply separately and *subtract* the products.

Example:

$9 \times (2 + 5) = (9 \times 2) + (9 \times 5)$

You can also use the Distributive Property of Multiplication for dividing, but *only* if the numbers you are adding or subtracting are in the **dividend**.

$(28 + 8) \div 4 = (28 \div 4) + (8 \div 4)$

You *cannot* use the Distributive Property when the numbers you are adding or subtracting are in the **divisor**.

$28 \div (4 + 2)$ *does not* $= (28 \div 4) + (28 \div 2)$

Identity Elements are numbers in a problem that do not affect the answer. When adding, the identity element is 0, because any addend or addends + 0 will not change the total.

In multiplication, the identity element is 1, because any factor or factors × 1 will not change the product.

However, subtraction and division do not have identity elements.

Remember...

Addition and multiplication both have identity elements. Division and subtraction do not have identity elements.

Exercises   SOLVE

1 $0 + 6 = 6$

2 $4 (4 + 3) = 28$
$4 \times 7 = 28$

3 $7 + 0 = 7$

4 $4 (2 + 3 + 4) = 36$
$4 \times 9 = 36$

5 $15 (7 + 3) = 150$
15×10

6 $6 (5 + 0) = 30$
$6 \times 5 = 30$

7 $3 \times 4 + 2 \times 9 = 30$
$12 + 18 = 30$

8 $(4 + 8) 4 = 48$
$12 \times 4 = 48$

9 $34 + 0 + 7 = 41$

10 $35 (2 + 3 + 0) = 175$
$35 \times 5 = 175$

11 $0 + 7 + 7 + 0 = 14$

12 $5 (33 - 11) =$
$5 \times 22 = 110$

13 $(64 - 28) 2 = 72$
$36 \times 2 = 72$

14 $7 - 0 + 0 - 7 = 0$
$7 - 0 = 7 + 0 = 7 - 7 = 0$

15 $8 (15 + 2 - 15) = 16$
$8 \times 2 = 16$

16.4

Zero Property, Equality Properties

Do numbers have any other properties?

Yes, and learning them will make studying mathematics easier.

Zero Property of Multiplication:

Any number $\times$ 0 = 0.

Remember that an equation is a mathematical statement that two things are equal.

$(6 + 4) = (9 + 1)$

Equality Property of Addition: You can keep an equation equal if you add *the same number* to both sides.

$(6 + 4) + 3 = (9 + 1) + 3$

Equality Property of Subtraction: You can keep an equation equal if you subtract *the same number* from both sides.

$(6 + 4) - 5 = (9 + 1) - 5$

Equality Property of Multiplication: You can keep an equation equal if you multiply both sides by *the same number.*

$(6 + 4) \times 10 = (9 + 1) \times 10$

Equality Property of Division: You can keep an equation equal if you divide both sides by *the same number*.

$(6 + 4) \div 2 = (9 + 1) \div 2$

Remember, you may never divide by 0.

Exercises   SOLVE

1 $5 \times 0 = $ 0

2 $0 (1 + 4) = $ 0

3 $0 \times 1.111 = $ 0

4 $7 (0 + 5) = $ 35

5 $0 \times 0 \times 3 \times 9 = $ 0

6 $233.31 \times 0 = $ 0

7 $0 \times 200.893 = $ 0

8 $0 \times 0 + 2 = $ 2

9 $0 (2 + 0) = $ 0

For questions 10–13, answer yes or no and briefly explain your answer.

10 If $8 + 1 = 6 + 3$ then does
$4 (8 + 1) = 4 (6 + 3)$?

_____

_____

11 If $6 \times 9 = 54$ then does
$4 + (6 \times 9) = 54 + 4$?

_____

_____

12 If $\frac{1}{5} = \frac{3}{15}$ then does
$\frac{1}{5} - 5 = \frac{3}{15} - 5$?

_____

_____

13 If $5 - 1 = 20 \times .2$ then does
$\frac{(5 - 1)}{22} = \frac{(20 \times .2)}{22}$?

_____

_____

Understanding Variable Expressions

Is there a way to solve a problem when one number is unknown? Yes, there is. You need to use **algebra**. Algebra is a branch of math you can use to find the value of unknown numbers. Unknown numbers are called **variables**.

To find the unknown number, or variable, you will probably have to use algebraic expressions. An **algebraic expression** is a group of variables, numbers, and operations.

Some Algebraic Expressions

$$s + 32 \qquad (k - 31) \times 3$$
$$(45 \div y) + 9 \qquad z^2$$
$$\frac{j}{3} \qquad 4g$$

The last expression means $4 \times g$. When you multiply a variable, you do not need to write the $\times$ sign. Instead, you just use a **coefficient**, which is a number that multiplies a variable.

Exercises   EXPLAIN

Put into words what each expression is describing.

1 $\dfrac{a}{4}$

_____

_____

2 $y + 3$

_____

_____

3 $4b + 8$

_____

_____

4 $.9q - 7$

_____

_____

5 $\dfrac{(x - 3)}{25}$

_____

_____

6 $8(2g + 6)$

_____

_____

7 $2n - 5$

_____

_____

8 $12(r - 14)$

_____

_____

9 $\dfrac{7}{h}$

_____

_____

10 $\dfrac{11 + b}{16}$

_____

_____

Solving Equations by Addition and Subtraction

How do you use addition and subtraction to solve algebraic expressions? Refer back to Lesson 16.4 where you learned the Equality Properties of Addition and Subtraction. These rules help you solve equations that use addition and subtraction.

In the first example, you subtract 6 from *both sides* of the equation to find *d*. In the second example, you add 4 to *both sides* of the equation to find *w*.

Examples:

$d + 6 = 20$ Find *d*. $w - 4 = 10$.   Find *w*.
$d = 12$ $w = 14$

Exercises SOLVE

Solve for the variable shown in the expression.

1 $x + 6 = 17$

2 $17 = s + 9$

3 $14 + z = 49$

4 $17 - f = 14$

5 $c - 11 = 11$

6 $y + 23 = 25$

7 $107 = 5 + l$

8 $k + 36 = 64$

9 $15 + u = 43$

10 $59 - t = 22$

11 $9 - a = 3$

12 $75 + b = 101$

13 $49 - e = 24$

14 $16 + d = 39$

15 $w + 15 = 81$

16 $q - 23 = 35$

Solving Equations by Multiplication and Division

Can you use the Equality Properties of Multiplication and Division to solve algebraic expressions, too? Yes you can. Before we look at these kinds of equations, you need to think about this: division and multiplication are opposites. If you multiply a number or a variable by a second number, and then you divide the product by that second number, you will end up with the original number or variable. For example: $7 \times 8 \div 8 = 7, h \div 2 \times 2 = h$. To solve a multiplication equation, divide both sides of the equation by the same number. To solve a division equation, multiply both sides of the equation by the same number.

Examples:

$9p = 45$. Find p. $\frac{u}{3} = 8$. Find u.

$p = 5$ $u = 24$

In the first example, you divide *both sides* of the equation by 9 to find p. In the second example, you multiply *both sides* of the equation by 3 to find u.

Remember...

You can keep an equation equal by performing the same operation on *both sides*.

Exercises **SOLVE**

1. $2y + 15 = 25$

2. $5 + 5p = 70$

3. $8c + 8 = 224$

4. $17 + \frac{w}{3} = 45$

5. $34 = 10 + 4q$

6. $42 = 7 + \frac{z}{5}$

7. $232 = 8 + 8x$

8. $63 = 3 + 4g$

9. $12 = \frac{g}{9}$

10. $3k + 5 = 56$

11. $49 = 10 + \frac{p}{5}$

12. $2y + 5 = 74$

13. $8d + 130 = 210$

14. $33 + \frac{1}{3}c = 66$

Name _Rushi*_

Negative Numbers

Are any numbers less than zero? Yes. They are called **negative numbers**. To show a negative number, put a minus sign in front of the number.

On this number line, a negative number falls to the left of zero, while a positive number falls to its right. 0 is neither positive nor negative.

Notice that both −4 and 4 are four spaces away from zero, but in opposite directions on the number line. We say that −4 is the **inverse** of 4, and vice versa.

The Property of Additive Inverses:
When you add a negative number to its inverse, the total is 0. For example: −34 + 34 = 0.

Number Line

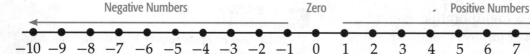

Negative Numbers   Zero   Positive Numbers

−10 −9 −8 −7 −6 −5 −4 −3 −2 −1 0 1 2 3 4 5 6 7 8 9 10

Exercises   ADD

1   (−4) + 4 = 0

_____

2   (−110) + 210 = 100

_____

3   (−9) + 17 + 9 + (−17) = 0

_____

4   145 + (−125) =
+20

_____

5   48 + (−38) =
10

_____

6   (−75) + 55 + 732 + (−712) =

_____

7 $\frac{1}{4} + (-\frac{1}{4}) =$

_____

8   541 + 641 + (−741) + (−641) =

_____

9   44 + (−77) + 0 =

_____

10 $16 + \frac{1}{4} + (-\frac{1}{4}) + (-10) =$

_____

Adding and Subtracting with Negative Numbers

Can you add and subtract negative numbers? Yes, but to do this you have to know about **absolute value**. Absolute value is the number without its sign. It represents the distance between the number and 0 on the number line.

Examples:

$$-10 + 7 = -3 \qquad -6 + 8 = 2$$
$$(-3) + (-8) = -11$$

Remember...

To subtract one negative number from another, change the second number to its inverse and *add*.

To add two negative numbers, add their absolute values, and put a minus sign in front of the total. To add a negative and a positive number, find their absolute values, then subtract the smaller one from the greater one. Your answer will have the same sign as the number with the greater absolute value.

Examples:

$(-6) - (+7)$	equals	$(-6) + (-7) = -13$
$(-3) - (-8) = 5$	equals	$(-3) + (+8) = 5$
$(-8) + (+3) = -5$	equals	$(-8) - (-3) = -5$

Exercises ADD

1. $17 + (-3) =$ _____

2. $(-15) + 6 =$ _____

3. $1 + (-12) =$ _____

4. $75 + (-36) =$ _____

5. $110 + (-56) + 14 =$ _____

6. $95 + (-65) + (-1) =$ _____

7. $(-20) + (-20) + 7 =$ _____

8. $51 + (-33) + 20 =$ _____

9. $30 + (-22) =$ _____

10. $18 + 18 + (-18) =$ _____

11. $(-25) + 14 =$ _____

12. $80 + 13 + 29 + (-100) =$ _____

13. $57 + (-39) + 10 =$ _____

14. $(-23) + 63 + (-9) =$ _____

15. $4 + 2 + (-7) + (-1) =$ _____

16. $1 + (-9) + 9 =$ _____

Name _____

Multiplying and Dividing with Negative Numbers

Negative numbers can also be multiplied and divided. You need to remember these two rules:

- When two numbers have the same sign, either negative or positive, their product or quotient is *positive*.

- When two numbers have different signs, one negative and one positive, their product or quotient is *negative*.

Examples:

$5 \times 4 = 20$	$(-5) \times (-4) = 20$
$(-5) \times 4 = -20$	$5 \times (-4) = -20$
$6 \div 2 = 3$	$(-6) \div (-2) = 3$
$(-6) \div 2 = -3$	$6 \div (-2) = -3$

Exercises   MULTIPLY OR DIVIDE

1 $5 \times (-3) =$ _____

2 $13 \times (-10) =$ _____

3 $100 \times (-1) =$ _____

4 $23 \times (-3) =$ _____

5 $15 \times (-15) =$ _____

6 $(-12) \times 20 =$ _____

7 $(-2) \times (-4) =$ _____

8 $(-1) \times 1 =$ _____

9 $(-125) \times (-1) =$ _____

10 $(-3) \times 103 =$ _____

11 $(-20) \div 20 =$ _____

12 $(-22) \times 0 =$ _____

13 $(-3) \times (-1) =$ _____

14 $(-12) \div 4 =$ _____

15 $15 \div (-3) =$ _____

16 $(-27) \div (-9 \div \frac{1}{9}) =$ _____

Plotting Ordered Pairs

Can you make a graph that uses number lines? Yes. You can use one number line horizontally as the *x*-axis, and one number line vertically as the *y*-axis. On a graph, two numbers can express a point. Each of the two numbers can be positive or negative. The first number locates the point on the *x*-axis. The second number locates the point on the *y*-axis.

Example:

In this example, Point A is written as (3,7). Point B is (−2,1). And Point C is (0,−5).

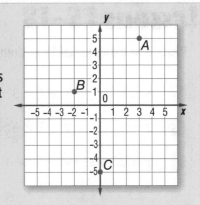

Exercises   PLOT ORDERED PAIRS

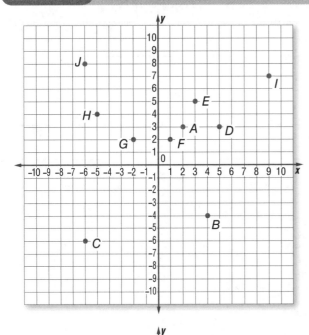

Give the coordinates for each point on the graph.

A _____   B _____

C _____   D _____

E _____   F _____

G _____   H _____

I _____   J _____

Plot the following ordered pairs on the graph:

A (3,2)   B (7,−7)

C (−7,−7)   D (−7,7)

E (7,7)   F (9,2)

G (6,7)   H (−8,−6)

I (−2,2)   J (−5,−5)

K (3,−4)   L (−2,−2)

Unit Test

Lessons 15–18

Restate in exponential form then calculate.

1 $8 \times 8 \times 2 + 3 \times 3 \times 3$ _____

2 $2 \times 2 \times 4 \times 4 - 3 \times 3 \times 3$ _____

3 $5 \times 25 \times 2 \times 2 \times 4 \times 4 + 7 \times 7 - 5 \times 5$ _____

Restate using scientific notation.

4 13,654,764.011 _____

5 28,397.01 _____

6 .100745 _____

7 21,194,668,041.1 _____

8 813.056 _____

Calculate using order of operations (PEMDAS).

9 $5 \times (7 - 3)^2 + (19 - 5) \times 2 + (6 - 3) \times 2 + 2^3$

10 $29 + (3 \times 5) \times 2 + (8 - 3)^2$

Calculate.

11 3^3 **12** 8^4 **13** $2^3 \times 2^{-2}$ **14** $10^{-8} \div 10^{-9}$ **15** $15^{11} \times 15^{-11}$

Unit Test

Lessons 15–18

What number property does each expression display?

16 $5 + (4 + 6) = (5 + 4) + 6$
_____

17 $2(6 + 3) = 2(6) + 2(3)$
_____

18 $15 + 16 + 18 = 18 + 16 + 15$
_____

19 $24(1) = 24$
_____

20 $8 + 0 = 8$
_____

21 $20 \times 1 = 20$
_____

22 $4 \times (5 \times 3) = (4 \times 5) \times 3$
_____

23 $63(0) + (63 + 0) = 0 + 63 = 63$
_____

Solve for x.

24 $6 + x = 13$

25 $x - 15 = 22$

26 $39 - x = 25$

27 $x + 60 = 90$

28 $6x + 3 = 33$

29 $4x - 5 = 19$

30 $6x + 3 = 45$

31 $2x + 14 = 42$

32 $4 - 4x = -48$

33 $\frac{x}{6} + 3 = 12$

34 $\frac{x}{2} - 5 = 30$

35 $\frac{1}{3}x - 4 = 16$

Solve each equation and indicate the point on the number line that corresponds with the answer.

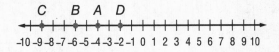

36 $-6 + 10 - 6 =$ _____

37 $-10 + 5 - 4 =$ _____

38 $-10 + (-4) + 8 =$ _____

39 $9 - 5 + (-8) =$ _____

Calculate.

40 -5×15

41 $-45 \div 9$

42 $63 \div (-7)$

43 $4 \times (-6) \div -3$

Lessons 15–18

Provide the ordered pairs for the points plotted on the graph.

44 A _____ **45** B _____

46 C _____ **47** D _____

48 E _____ **49** F _____

50 G _____ **51** H _____

52 I _____ **53** J _____

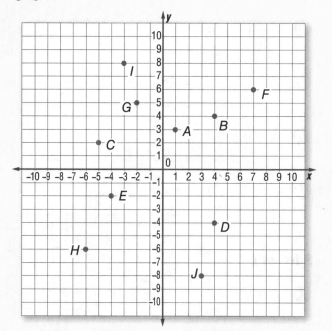

Plot the following points on the grid provided:

54 A (1,4)

55 B (4,1)

56 C (3,9)

57 D (−9,−3)

58 E (−4,4)

59 F (−1,−4)

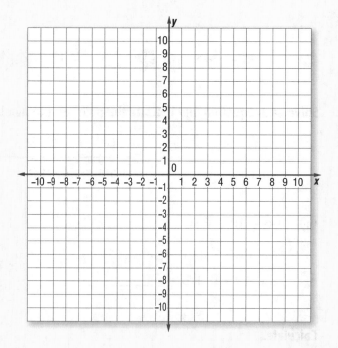

Customary Units of Length

Length is customarily measured in inches (in.), feet (ft), yards (yd), and miles (mi). You can compare them to each other, and even change one to another by simple calculations.

1 foot = 12 in.

1 yard = 3 ft

1 mile = 1,760 yd or 5,280 ft

Exercises **CALCULATE**

1 12.5 feet is how many yards? _____

2 1 mile is how many feet? _____

3 144 inches is how many yards? _____

4 3 miles is how many yards? _____

5 128 inches is how many feet? _____

6 10,560 yards is how many miles?_____

7 15.5 yards is how many feet? _____

8 3.25 miles is how many inches? _____

9 31.5 yards is how many inches? _____

10 25 miles is how many yards? _____

11 42,931 feet is how many miles? _____

12 52 feet is how many inches? _____

13 345 yards is how many feet? _____

14 63,360 inches is how many miles? _____

15 31,680 inches is how many miles? _____

16 7,000 yards is how many inches? _____

17 1,590 feet is how many yards? _____

18 500 miles is how many yards? _____

Customary Units of Liquid Volume

When you buy a fruit juice or when you add a liquid to a recipe, you often measure in units of **liquid volume**. Liquid volume is the amount of liquid a container can hold. Liquid volume is measured in cups (c), pints (pt), quarts (qt) and gallons (gal). And, as with units of length, you can compare these units to each other, and change one to another by simple calculations.

1 pint = 2 cups

1 quart = 2 pints

1 gallon = 4 quarts

Exercises   CALCULATE

1 4 gallons is how many pints?

8 _____

2 A 33-gallon gas tank has how many quarts? _____

3 64 quarts is how many gallons?

16 _____

4 36 pints is how many gallons?

_____

5 2,000 cups is how many quarts?

_____

6 300 pints is how many cups?

_____

7 64 gallons is how many pints?

_____

8 42 quarts is how many cups?

_____

9 64 pints is how many gallons?

_____

10 132 pints is how many quarts?

_____

11 250 cups is how many pints?

_____

12 175 pints is how many cups?

_____

13 88 gallons is how many quarts?

_____

14 42 pints is how many gallons?

_____

15 384 quarts is how many gallons?

_____

16 225 cups is how many pints?

_____

Customary Units of Weight

Weight is customarily measured in ounces (oz), pounds (lb), and tons (T). As with units of length and liquid volume, you can compare units of weight to each other, and change one to another by simple calculations.

1 pound = 16 oz   1 ton = 2,000 lb

Exercises   CALCULATE

1 20 pounds is how many ounces?

_____

2 5.2 tons is how many pounds?

_____

3 4 tons is how many ounces?

_____

4 196 ounces is how many pounds?

_____

5 3.5 tons is how many pounds?

_____

6 1,600 pounds is how many tons?

_____

7 1.5 tons is how many ounces?

_____

8 680 ounces is how many pounds?

_____

9 3.2 tons is how many pounds?

_____

10 48,000 ounces is how many tons?

_____

11 65.2 lbs is how many ounces?

_____

12 80,000 ounces is how many tons?

_____

13 Three 200-pound men weigh how many tons?

_____

14 A 13.5-ton elephant weighs how many pounds?

_____

15 A $1\frac{3}{4}$ ton truck can carry $1\frac{3}{4}$ of a ton of materials in its bed. How many pounds is that?

_____

16 If there are 1,050 students at school and each eats 3 ounces of turkey burger for lunch, how many pounds of turkey burger is that?

_____

Perimeter

Imagine that you want to find the distance around a figure. This is the **perimeter**.

Example:

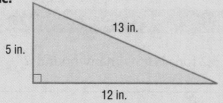

The perimeter of this triangle is
$5 + 12 + 13 = 30$ in.

You could change this total number into feet by dividing the number of inches by 12.

$$\frac{30}{12} = 2\frac{1}{2} \text{ ft}$$

Example:

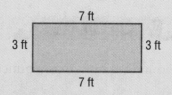

The perimeter of this rectangle is
$7 + 3 + 7 + 3 = 20$ ft.

You could change this total into inches by multiplying by 12.

$20 \times 12 = 240$ inches

Remember...

Right triangles are usually marked with a special symbol.

Exercises SOLVE

1. Which has a longer perimeter, a triangle with sides of 26 feet or a hexagon with sides of 18 feet?

   _____

2. If Trent walks east for 25 feet, then north for 30 feet, then west for 25 feet, how long would he have to walk to get to his starting point and how long did he walk in total?

   _____

3. If you have a 120-foot piece of fencing wire, how long would each side of a square-shaped corral be if all the fencing is used?

   _____

4. If you want to put a ribbon around a rectangular box with sides of 5 and 10 inches, how much ribbon would you need?

   _____

5. What is the perimeter of the figure shown?

   52

   _____

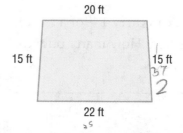

Name _____

Area

To calculate a figure's **area**, you need to know what to call those units. The units used in describing area are: square inches, square feet, square yards, or even square miles. Remember, however, that a square foot does *not* equal 12 square inches; and a square yard does *not* equal 3 square feet; and a square mile does *not* equal 1,760 square yards.

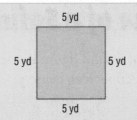

5 yd × 5 yd = 25 sq yd

A square is a special kind of rectangle, with all of its sides equal in length.

You may remember that a number to the second power, or a number multiplied once by itself, is called "squared."

Examples:

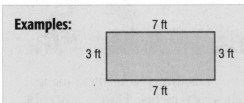

7 ft × 3 ft = 21 square ft

The area of a rectangle is its length (*l*) × its width (*w*).

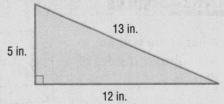

$\frac{1}{2}$ × 5 in. × 12 in. = 30 sq in.

The area of a triangle is $\frac{1}{2}$ × its base (*b*) × its height (*h*).

Exercises   SOLVE

1 How many people can you allow on a beach if the lifeguards want to have 30 sq ft per person and the beach is 1,000 ft long and 200 ft wide? Round to a whole number.

_____

2 A square that has sides of 25 ft is split in half down the middle. What is the area of each of the pieces?

_____

3 A right triangle has a base of 24 feet and a height of 7 feet. What is its area?

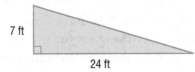

_____

4 Which has a larger area, a triangle with a base of 15 ft and a height of 25 ft or a square with sides of 14 ft?

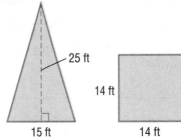

_____

19.6

Volume of a Solid

The **volume** of a solid figure is measured by
cubic inches, cubic feet, cubic yards, and cubic miles.

Example:

To find the volume of a rectangular solid, multiply
length × width × height (*h*).

Volume = 5 yd × 2 yd × 3 yd = 30 **cu yd**

Volume of a rectangular pyramid = $\frac{1}{3}$ × Base Area × Height

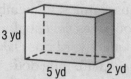
3 yd, 5 yd, 2 yd

Exercises   SOLVE

1 What is the volume
of a cube with sides of
10 inches?

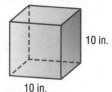
10 in.
10 in.

2 A shoe box has dimensions of 12 inches
by 8 inches by 6 inches. How many cubic
feet is it?

3 A rectangular solid with sides of 9 ft by 5
ft by 13 ft has what volume?

4 A cube that has sides of 120 inches has
how many cubic yards of volume?

5 A storage container in the form of a
rectangular solid has dimensions of
12 inches by 30 inches by 16 inches. If
a pound of sugar takes up $\frac{1}{4}$ sq ft, how
many pounds of sugar can you put in the
container?

6 A parking lot measures 420 ft long and
162 ft wide. If a construction company is
told that it needs to have 3 feet of asphalt
under the parking lot for proper drainage,
how many cubic yards do they need to
order?

Time

You know how to tell time, but have you ever thought about the units you use to tell time?

Remember that some months have different overall lengths. Some months have 30 days, while others have 31. February has only 28 days, except in a leap year, when it is 29 days long. Because of the extra day added to February, a leap year has 366 days.

A few other terms you need to know to talk about time:

a.m. = *ante meridiem*, "before the middle of the day"

The middle of the day is noon, so a.m. hours are between midnight and noon.

p.m. = *post meridiem*, "after the middle of the day"

Those hours are between noon and midnight.

1 minute = 60 seconds	1 hour = 60 minutes	1 day = 24 hours
1 week = 7 days = 1 month = 28, 29, 30, or 31 days		
1 year = 12 months = 52 weeks = 365 (or 366) days		
1 decade = 10 years		1 century = 100 years

Exercises   CALCULATE

1 36 hours = _____ seconds

2 25 days = _____ hours

3 35 days = _____ minutes

4 96 hours = _____ days

5 32 days = _____ minutes

6 125 minutes = _____ hours

7 91 days = _____ weeks

8 300 years = _____ decades

9 2,500 years = _____ centuries

10 6,000 seconds = _____ weeks

11 If you get paid $700 and you worked 3.2 days, approximately how much did you make per hour (assume an 8-hour day of work)?

_____

12 The production rate for widgets in the factory is 8 per second. How many widgets should you make in a 9-hour shift?

_____

13 What is the maximum of different centuries that a person can live in if he lived to be 110 years?

_____

14 If you get paid $8.00 per hour and you work 5,400 minutes, how much will you earn?

_____

Name _____

Metric Units of Length

You may have heard of metric units. In America, we do not usually measure with these units, but they are much easier to work with mathematically than customary units. That is because metric units are all based on the powers of 10. The metric units of length are millimeters (mm), centimeters (cm), meters (m), and kilometers (km).

Remember...

To make calculations simpler for yourself, learn these prefixes:

milli = thousandth   centi = hundredth   kilo = thousand

1 centimeter = 10 mm	1 meter = 100 cm	1 km = 1000 m

Exercises CALCULATE

1 335 cm = _____ m

2 6235 mm = _____ m

3 5.761 km = _____ cm

4 725.02 km = _____ mm

5 335 cm + 550 mm = _____ m

6 2.611 km = _____ cm

7 12 cm + 12 mm = _____ m

8 6.872 m = _____ mm

9 8 km + 65 m = _____ m

10 320 km + 415 m = _____ cm

11 478.98 cm + 760.34 cm = _____ m

12 540 cm = _____ km

13 45 m + 35 cm = _____ cm

14 76 m + .355 m = _____ mm

15 1.1755 km = _____ m

16 66.66 cm + 666 mm + 66 m = _____ m

17 2104 m = _____ km

18 1545 cm = _____ km

Metric Units of Liquid Volume

The basic metric unit of liquid volume is the liter (L.) There are also milliliters (mL) and kiloliters (kL).

1 liter = 1000 mL
1 kiloliter = 1000 L

Exercises   CALCULATE

1 2.1 L = _____ mL

2 1700 L = _____ kL

3 3.456 L = _____ mL

4 350 L = _____ mL

5 3.901 kL = _____ mL

6 161.34 mL = _____ L

7 767 mL = _____ kL

8 1276 mL + 487 L = _____ L

9 2 kL + 135 L = _____ L

10 71 mL + 141 L = _____ kL

11 835 kL + 4500 L = _____ kL

12 562 kL + 5213 L = _____ kL

13 423.98 L + 875.23 mL = _____ L

14 141.3 L − 43.2 mL = _____ mL

15 A $\frac{3}{4}$ liter bottle of water is a common size. How many of these bottles of water would it take to fill a 20-liter container?

_____

16 If the reservoir has 200,000,000,000 centiliters of water in it, how many kiloliters does it contain?

_____

17 If you are providing beverages for 25 students and family members at the school outing and each person expects to drink 1,500 centiliters, how many liters of beverages will you need?

_____

18 If an aquarium holds 60 liters of water, and each cup of water holds 250 milliliters, how many cups of water does the aquarium hold?

_____

Name _____

Metric Units of Mass

The basic metric unit of mass is the gram (g).
Remember the prefixes milli- = thousandth,
centi- = hundredth, and kilo- = thousand.

| 1 cg = 10 mg |
| 1 g = 100 cg |
| 1 kg = 1000 g |

Remember...

Metric units of mass are easy to work with because
they are also based on the powers of ten.

Exercises CALCULATE

1 200 g = _____ kg

2 125 kg = _____ mg

3 660 g = _____ kg

4 4500 mg = _____ g

5 11.3 kg = _____ mg

6 300 mg = _____ g

7 500 g + 600 mg = _____ g

8 7 kg + 190 g = _____ cg

9 438 g + 1.62 kg = _____ g

10 267 kg − 133 g = _____ kg

11 354 g − 346 mg = _____ g

12 4300 g + 3300 mg = _____ kg

13 5300 g − 2430 mg = _____ g

14 12.34 kg + 1.66 kg = _____ g

15 2 mg + 4 g + 5 kg = _____ kg

16 300 kg + 300 g + 300 cg = _____ mg

17 142 g + 258 mg = _____ cg

18 65 g + 6500 g = _____ kg

Metric Perimeter, Area, and Volume of a Solid

You can use metric units to calculate perimeters, areas, and the volumes of solids. You have to remember that you are working with metric units, and your answers will be expressed in metric units.

Perimeter is expressed in mm, cm, m, or km.

Area is expressed in sq mm, sq cm, sq m, or sq km.

The volume of a solid is expressed in cu mm, cu cm, cu m, or cu km.

Remember...
Do not change from metric to customary units.
For example, 1 **sq km** *does not* = 1,000 **sq miles**

Exercises   CALCULATE

1 What is the perimeter of a square with sides of 7 cm?

_____

What is the area?

_____

7 cm
7 cm

2 The perimeter of this figure with 6 equal sides is 48 millimeters. What is the length of each side?

_____

3 A cube has sides of 6 cm. What is the volume of the cube?

_____

What is the surface area of the whole figure?

_____

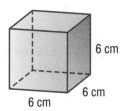
6 cm
6 cm
6 cm

4 A rectangle has sides of 2.4 cm and 8 cm. What is the perimeter of the rectangle?

_____

What is the area of the rectangle?

_____

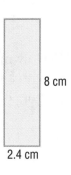
8 cm
2.4 cm

5 What is the perimeter of this rectangle with sides of 14 meters and 6 meters?

_____

What is the area?

_____

14 m
6 m

6 Damian designed a course around his neighborhood to race his bicycle with friends. His neighborhood is in the shape of a regular pentagon with 5 equal sides measuring 500 meters each. If Damian can ride his bicycle at a speed of 20 km per hour, how many times around the course will he go in an hour?

_____

7 Anabelle is buying a new rug for her living room. The rug store prices the rug by the square meter. If Anabelle needs a rug with dimensions of 3.7 meters long and 2 meters wide, and the rug store charges $12.00 per square meter, how much will she pay for a new rug?

_____

What is the perimeter of the rug?

_____

8 What is the volume of the rectangular solid?

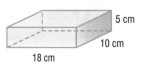

_____

9 What is the area of the triangle?

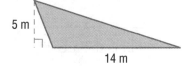

_____

10 How much water can a swimming pool with a flat bottom hold? It is 12 meters long, 8 meters wide, and 2.5 meters deep.

_____

11 What is the area of the triangle?

_____

12 What is the area of this rectangle?

_____

Name _____

Temperature

The units used to describe temperature are called degrees. Degrees are written with a small circle to the top right of a number: 30 degrees = 30°. Customary degrees are measured on the **Fahrenheit** scale. You must add the word Fahrenheit (or just **F**), because other temperature scales that are *not* customary are also used to describe temperature.

The metric unit to describe temperature is called the **Celsius** degree (or just **C**). This is also sometimes referred to as **Centigrade**.

Celsius	Fahrenheit	
0° C	32° F	Freezing point of water
100° C	212° F	Boiling point of water
35° C	95° F	Hot air temperature
37° C	98.6° F	Human body temperature

The Celsius scale is used in scientific work and is easier to use than the Fahrenheit scale. Even though both are expressed in degrees, a Celsius degree *does not* equal a Fahrenheit degree!

You can change Celsius to Fahrenheit temperatures, or Fahrenheit to Celsius temperatures. To do so, you must use the following equations:

$$(F - 32) \times \left(\frac{5}{9}\right) = C \qquad C \times \left(\frac{9}{5}\right) + 32 = F$$

Example:

Convert 98.6° F to Celsius.

Step 1: Set up the equation:
$$(98.6 - 32) \times \left(\frac{5}{9}\right) = C$$

Step 2: Calculate: $66.6 \times \dfrac{5}{9} = 37$
$$98.6° F = 37° C$$

Exercises   CONVERT

1 200° C = _____ F

2 132° F = _____ C

3 81° F = _____ C

4 32° C = _____ F

5 214° F = _____ C

6 320° F = _____ C

7 10° F = _____ C

8 45° C = _____ F

9 75° F = _____ C

10 90° C = _____ F

11 −15° F = _____ C

12 130° F = _____ C

13 37° C = _____ F

14 2000° C = _____ F

15 244° C = _____ F

16 Sarah has a fever and is running a temperature of 39° C. What is her temperature in Fahrenheit?

_____

17 Jared is baking cookies for a bake sale. His recipe calls for him to set the oven to a temperature of 350° F. If his oven only displays temperature in Celsius, then to what temperature should Jared set his oven?

_____

Name _____

Changing from Customary Units to Metric Units

Can you change customary units to metric units? Yes. Here are a few charts to guide you. Keep in mind that some of the metric units are not exact, but they are fairly close.

Length	Liquid Volume	Weight or Mass
1 inch = 2.54 centimeters	1 cup = .237 liters	1 ounce = 28.35 grams
1 foot = .305 meters	1 pint = .473 liters	1 pound = .454 kilograms
1 yard = .914 meters	1 quart = .946 liters	1 ton = 907.18 kilograms
1 mile = 1.609 kilometers	1 gallon = 3.785 liters	
	1 fluid ounce = 29.574 milliliters	

Exercises CONVERT

1 The weight limit on a bridge is 16,000 pounds. What is the weight limit in kilograms?

_____

2 The directions on a plant fertilizer bag recommend using 3 pounds for a 4 × 10 garden. How many grams is that?

_____

3 A 2-ton truck weighs how many kilograms?

_____

4 A car with a 23-gallon gas tank holds how many liters of gas?

_____

5 A 24-ounce fruit juice bottle contains how many liters of fluid?

_____

6 Jasmine has a 150-ft length of rope. Does she have enough rope to reach the bottom of a 40-meter cliff?

_____

7 A 3-pound lobster weighs how many kilograms?

_____

8 Would you rather have 2.4 pounds or 1,000 grams of gold?

_____

9 About how many meters tall is a 100-ft tree?

_____

10 How many meters tall is a 9.5-foot tree?

_____

Changing from Metric Units to Customary Units

Since customary units can be changed to metric units, you can obviously reverse this process. Again, remember that some of the numbers on the charts below are not exact. However, they are fairly close.

Length	Liquid Volume	Weight or Mass
1 millimeter = .039 inches 1 centimeter = .394 inches 1 meter = 39.37 inches 1 kilometer = .621 miles	1 liter = 1.056 quarts 1 kiloliter = 263.2 gallons	1 gram = .035 ounces 1 kilogram = 2.205 pounds

Exercises CONVERT

1 If each person on a hike is supposed to carry 1.75 liters of water, how many gallons of water would you need to bring for a group of 45 people?

_____

2 Every camper is served .15 kilograms of cereal each morning. If there are 12 campers, how many pounds of cereal will you need to bring for a 7-day trip?

_____

3 11 kilograms is about how many ounces?

_____

4 A 3-meter diving board is how many feet above the pool?

_____

5 A 15-meter length of rope is how many feet long?

_____

6 A dog weighs 22 kilograms. How many pounds is that?

_____

7 A 50-meter pool is the standard size for the Olympics. What is that length in feet?

_____

8 A reservoir contains 11,250,000 kiloliters of water. How many gallons is that?

_____

9 The local middle school sponsored a 6-kilometer race for everyone to run. What is the length of the race in miles?

_____

10 A jet that travels at 4,200 kilometers per hour is traveling how many miles per hour?

_____

11 How many inches is 300 centimeters?

_____

How many feet?

_____

12 The average defensive lineman on the football team at Bloomingdale High School weighs 110 kilograms. The average offensive lineman weighs 240 pounds. Which position has a lower average weight?

_____

1 Armando is going to replace the trim around all of the doors in his house. The outside of each door measures $18\frac{1}{2}$ feet. If he has 9 doors, how many inches of trim does he need to replace?

_____

2 Ashley wants to empty her fish tank before she cleans it. The fish tank holds 34 gallons. She is using a one-quart container to empty the tank by hand. How many full containers will she need to empty the tank?

_____

3 Annika weighed boxes for shipping books to customers. The first box weighed 160 ounces, the second box weighed $10\frac{3}{8}$ pounds, and the third box weighed $\frac{1}{200}$ ton. Which box weighed the most?

_____

4 Mandie wants to fence in her corral, and needs to know how much fencing to purchase. The corral has an irregular shape, with sides of $25\frac{1}{4}$ feet, 330 inches, 6 yards, one foot, $\frac{3}{160}$ of a mile, and 9 feet. How much fence material will she need?

_____ feet

5 What is the area of a rectangle with a length of 20 ft and a width of 144 inches?

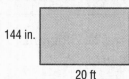

144 in.

20 ft

_____ square feet

6 What is the area of a right triangle with sides of 6 feet, 8 feet, and 120 inches?

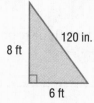

120 in.

8 ft

6 ft

_____ square feet

7 What is the volume of a rectangular box with sides of 48 inches and $3\frac{1}{2}$ feet, and a height of 30 inches?

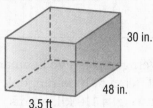

30 in.

48 in.

3.5 ft

_____ cubic feet

8 A modern spacecraft must travel 8.1 miles per second in order to reach the planet Mars. How far does the spacecraft travel in a minute?

_____

in an hour? _____

in a day? _____

Lessons 19–21

9 If the distance to the moon from earth is 248,000 miles, how long does it take the spacecraft in the previous exercise to travel to the moon? _____

How many times a day could the spacecraft go back and forth between the moon and the earth?

_____

10 The world record for the shot put is 23.12 meters. The world record for the discus throw is 74.08 meters. How many centimeters longer is the record for the discus throw than the record for the shot put?

_____

11 Stacey is measuring fabric for her grandmother, who is going to make a rectangular banner for the school. The banner will be 6.5 meters in length and 2,350 millimeters in width. How much fabric will Stacey's grandmother need to buy?

_____ sq cm

12 Sharon has three cans of latex paint to recycle. One can holds 2,957 milliliters of paint, the second can holds 105.6 centiliters of paint, and the third can holds 3.9 liters of paint. How much paint, in total, will Sharon be recycling?

_____ liters

13 What is the area of a triangle with sides of 8 cm, 8 cm, a base of 4 cm, and a height of 6 cm?

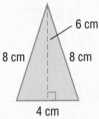

8 cm   6 cm   8 cm

4 cm

_____ sq cm

14 Jerrie walked around the entire rectangular school parking lot, which measures 106 meters by 7,500 centimeters. How far did Jerrie walk?

_____ meters

15 How much topsoil can fit into a rectangular dump truck that measures 3.6 meters in width, 6.5 meters in length, and 3.5 meters high?

_____ cu meters

16 The average player on the soccer team measures 5 feet, 11 inches tall. About how tall is that in centimeters?

_____

17 The average taxicab has a gas tank that holds 85 liters of gasoline. How much is that in quarts?

_____ quarts

In gallons?

_____ gallons

18 Pauline surveyed her neighborhood and found that the average house measured 55 feet by 32 feet by 20 feet tall. What is the total outside surface area in square feet?

_____ sq ft

In square yards? _____ sq yds

19 A body temperature of 103.6° F is considered an extremely high fever. What temperature is that in Celsius?

_____

20 In track and field, the standard middle distance event is the 5,000 meters. About how many feet is 5,000 meters?

_____ feet

21 What is the volume of the rectangular pyramid?

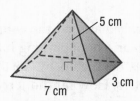

22 What is the volume of the triangular solid?

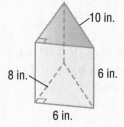

23 The air conditioning company suggests that people keep the temperature in their homes between 23 and 26 degrees Celsius during the summer. What is that range in degrees Fahrenheit?

_____

24 The distance of a flight from Boston to Chicago is about 1,200 miles. The average ground speed for a commercial airliner is about 850 kilometers per hour. About how long will it take to fly from Boston to Chicago?

_____ hours

Points and Lines

You have probably used the words "point" and "line" before, but do those terms have mathematical meanings?

You probably think of a point as a dot, which is what we mean when we use "point" in everyday use. However, a **point** in mathematics is a specific location in space. It has no dimensions at all. Each point is usually labeled with a capital letter.

A **line** is a perfectly straight path of points. It goes in both directions, and it never ends. When we draw a line, we use a pencil so we can see it. However, a line in mathematics has only one dimension, length.

Since a line is a path of points, it can be named by *any* two points located *anywhere* on it, and you can use those points in either order. So in the illustration above, Line YZ = Line ZY, and Line WX = Line XW.

Intersecting lines cross each other at a specific point. In this example, Lines YZ and WX cross at Point U.

Exercises   IDENTIFY

1 List the points located in the figure below.

_____

2 How many different points are located in the figure below?

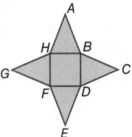

_____

3 Do the figures for exercises 1 and 2 contain any lines? Why or why not?

_____

_____

_____

4 List all possible names for the line pictured below.

_____

Name _____

Line Segments and Rays

If lines go on forever in both directions, can you talk about a line that ends at one or both sides? Yes, and you may have guessed that there are some mathematical terms for these.

S •——————• T

A **line segment** is a specific part of a line that has ends at two points. It is named by its two endpoints. So segment ST = segment TS. We can write it this way:

$$\overline{ST} = \overline{TS}$$

Q •——————•→ R

A **ray** is a part of a line that begins at a specific point, called a **vertex**, or **endpoint**. The line then extends from there in one direction without coming to an end. To define a ray, you must use one other letter along the line's path—but remember that the second letter is *not* the line's end. The *first* point in the name of a ray is its vertex. So ray QR *does not* equal ray RQ. Ray QR has a different vertex from ray RQ, and goes in the opposite direction!

$$\overrightarrow{QR} \neq \overleftarrow{RQ}$$

Exercises   IDENTIFY

1 How many line segments are there if you connect all the vertexes in this figure? Some, but not all, have been connected for you.

_____

2 Let A stand for the town Augusta, and B stand for the town Bar Harbor. Using these two letters, what would be the ray if you were traveling from Bar Harbor through Augusta?

_____

3 Name all the possible line segments in this figure.

_____

_____

4 At right is a drawing of an airport runway. Name all the possible rays that could be used to describe the different ways a plane could take off. For points, use the numbers at the end of the runways: 15, 24, 8 and 33. An example of one is ray 15 − 33. Name the other three.

_____

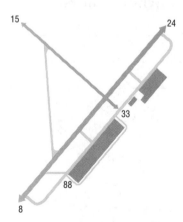

Measuring Angles

Rays from two intersecting lines can meet at the same vertex. When they do, they form an **angle**, which is named by both its lines. The vertex is in the middle of the name.

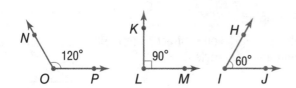

Rays NO and OP intersect at point O, the vertex of each line, to form angle NOP.

You measure angles in degrees. A straight line is 180°, so angles are always smaller than 180°. If an angle is greater than 90°, it is an **obtuse angle**. If it is less than 90°, it is an **acute angle**. If it is *exactly* 90°, it is a **right angle**, which is often shown with a small square inside the angle.

∠NOP is an obtuse angle. ∠KLM is a right angle. ∠HIJ is an acute angle.

Exercises   IDENTIFY

Label the angles as acute, obtuse, or right.

1   63°   _____

2   123°   _____

3   90°   _____

4   23°   _____

5   93°   _____

6   80°   _____

7   90°   ∠DEF = _____

8   130°   ∠RST = _____

9   105°   ∠LMN = _____

10   50°   ∠QRS = _____

11   35°   ∠ABC = _____

12   155°   ∠GHI = _____

Types of Angles

Angles always measure fewer degrees than a straight line. Two angles can be added together to form 180°, or a straight line.

Two angles that form a line are called **supplementary angles**. Their sum will equal 180°. So if you know the measurement of one angle, you can figure out the measurement of the other angle. Notice that a single letter placed near the vertex can sometimes be used to identify angles.

Example:

If ∠F = 75°, you subtract this value from 180°.
180 − 75 equals angle G.
Angle G = 105°.

Angles have other kinds of relationships, too. Two acute angles that form a right angle are called **complementary angles**. The sum of these two angles equals 90°.

Example:

If ∠E = 35°, you subtract 35 from 90 to find angle D. Angle D = 55°.

Two intersecting lines will always form four angles. The angles opposite each other are called **vertical angles**, and they are equal.
∠A = ∠C. ∠B = ∠D.

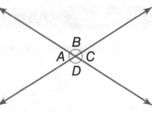

Exercises   IDENTIFY

1 What is the measure of angle Q?

_____

2 What is the measure of angle Z?

_____

3 Identify the supplementary angles in the figure below.

_____

4 The measure of ∠G is given. Determine the measure of the remaining angles.

_____

Name _____

Types of Angles (cont.)

There is a simple way to prove that vertical angles are equal.

∠A and ∠B form a straight line.
So ∠B = 180° − ∠A.

∠B and ∠C also form a straight line.
∠B = 180° − ∠C.

Therefore ∠A = ∠C

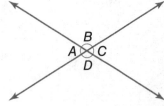

Exercises   SOLVE

1 From this figure, give examples of two complementary, two supplementary, and two vertical angles.

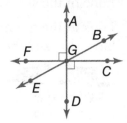

Complementary _____

_____

Supplementary _____

_____

Vertical _____

_____

2 For the figure below, list all complementary and supplementary angles.

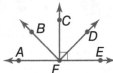

Complementary _____

_____

Supplementary _____

_____

3

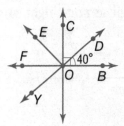

Are angle DOB and angle DOC complementary? _____

Explain. _____

_____

_____

4 Identify the measure of the angles in this figure.

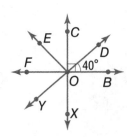

COD _____

COF _____

FOY _____

YOX _____

FOX _____

Name _____

Triangles

You know that a 2-dimensional figure with three sides is called a **triangle**. The three angles in a triangle add up to 180°.

acute triangle   right triangle   obtuse triangle

All triangles have at least two angles that are acute. In an **acute triangle**, *all* three angles are acute. In a **right triangle**, one of the angles is a right angle. In an **obtuse triangle**, one of the angles is obtuse. Because all three of its angles add up to 180°, a triangle can have only one angle that measures 90° or more.

equilateral triangle   isosceles triangle   scalene triangle

Another way of looking at triangles is to look at the length of their sides. In an **equilateral triangle**, all three sides are the same length. They are **congruent**, or equal. In an **isosceles triangle**, two sides are congruent, but the third side is not. In a **scalene triangle**, none of the sides are congruent.

Look at the red marks on some of the triangles. Sides marked the same way are congruent.

Remember...

Right angles are usually marked with a special symbol:

Exercises   IDENTIFY

Label the triangle as acute, right, or obtuse.

1
55°
80° 45°

_____

2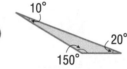
10°
20°
150°

_____

3
x°
40°

_____

4
A b H
c a
B

_____

5
60°
60° 60°

_____

6
120°
30° 30°

_____

Label the triangle as equilateral, isosceles, or scalene.

7

_____

8
60° 60°

_____

9

_____

Name _____

Quadrilaterals

Can you name a 2-dimensional figure with 4 angles? A 2-dimensional figure with four angles—and four sides—is called a **quadrilateral**.

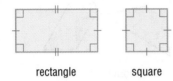

rectangle   square

You probably already recognize a **rectangle**, which has four right angles. A rectangle's opposite sides are parallel and the same length. If *all* four sides of a rectangle are the same length, it is a **square**.

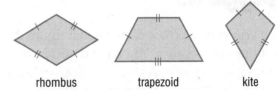

rhombus   trapezoid   kite

Like a rectangle, the opposite sides of a **rhombus** are parallel and have the same length. Unlike a rectangle, a rhombus does *not* have four right angles.

A **trapezoid** has two opposite sides that are parallel, but they are *not* the same length. The other two sides of a trapezoid are *not* parallel.

If a quadrilateral looks like a typical toy kite, it's called a **kite**. Two of its angles are equal. Its longer two *touching* sides are equal in length, and so are its shorter two *touching* sides.

Exercises   IDENTIFY

Label the shape as: square, rectangle, rhombus, trapezoid, or kite.

1   2.5 m
2.5 m [square] 2.5 m
2.5 m

_____

2   45° 45°

_____

3

_____

4

_____

5

_____

6

_____

7

_____

8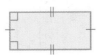

_____

9   6 in.   6 in.
6 in.

_____

Name _____

Polygons

Have you ever seen a 2-dimensional figure that has more than 4 sides? You have if you have ever seen a stop sign. A stop sign is an octagon, an 8-sided **polygon**. A polygon is a closed 2-dimensional figure made up of line segments. In fact, triangles and quadrilaterals are polygons, too. However, mathematicians usually don't call a figure a polygon unless it has more than 3 sides. The most common polygons are named for the number of their sides.

pentagon   hexagon   heptagon   octagon

penta = 5, **hexa** = 6, **hepta** = 7, **octa** = 8

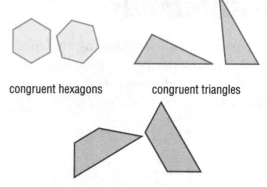

congruent hexagons   congruent triangles

not congruent trapezoids

If two polygons have exactly the same shape, size, and angles, then they are congruent. Congruent polygons do *not* have to face in the same direction. So do *not* trust your eyes. The best way to tell if two polygons are congruent is to measure the sides and angles of both.

To find the perimeter of a polygon, add the lengths of its sides.

Exercises   IDENTIFY

Label the polygons.

1   **2**   **3**   **4**

_____   _____   _____   _____

5   **6**   **7**   **8**

_____   _____   _____   _____

9 Are these two figures congruent? Why or why not?

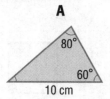

A   B

80°   40° 10 cm
60°   80°
10 cm

_____

_____

10 Are these two figures congruent? Why or why not?

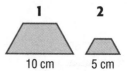

1   2

10 cm   5 cm

_____

_____

Circles

There are some special terms you need to know when describing circles. The distance around a circle is called its **circumference**. Every point on a circle's circumference is an equal distance from the circle's center point, or **origin**.

A **radius** is a line segment that begins at a circle's origin and extends to its circumference. In a circle, all radii (plural of "radius") are equal in length.

A line segment that has both its endpoints on the circumference is called a **chord**. If a chord passes through the origin, it is called a **diameter**. The length of a circle's diameter is two times the length of the circle's radius.

Exercises   IDENTIFY

1 What is the radius of the circle?

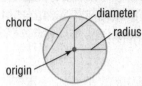

_____

2 What is the radius of the circle?

10 cm

_____

3 Identify the 2 radii and the one chord below.

_____

4 Identify the radius and chord in the figure below.

_____

5 What are the 5 chords formed by inscribing the pentagon inside of the circle below?

_____
_____

6 Using the letters provided, can the diameter in the figure below be named? Explain your answer.

_____
_____

Name _____

Circles (cont.)

Pi (π) is the Greek letter that stands for a very long decimal used to calculate a circle's circumference and area. Pi is the ratio of a circle's diameter to its circumference. Pi is exactly the same ratio for every circle. Sometimes the decimal is rounded to 3.14, but most mathematicians just use π to stand for it.

The circumference of a circle = pi times its diameter (πd).

The area of a circle = pi times the square of its radius = πr^2.

Remember to express area in square units. For example, square inches, square feet, square yards, and so on.

Exercises   IDENTIFY

7 How many ways can you describe the radius in this circle?

_____

8 Which two lines in the circle below are chords?

_____

9 Identify the chord and the diameter below.

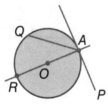

_____

10 Calculate the area of the circle below. Leave your answer in the form of pi.

10 in.

_____

Calculate the circumference and the area.

10

11 Circumference = _____

Area = _____

7

12 Circumference = _____

Area = _____

Surface Area of Solid Figures

Not all figures are 2-dimensional. Can you name some common 3-dimensional—or **solid**—figures?

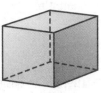

cube

You need to learn some new terms:

Face: A flat surface of a solid figure. Each face looks like a 2-dimensional figure.

Edge: The line at which two faces meet.

Vertex (of a Solid): A specific point at which *more than* 2 faces meet or where a curve originates.

Base: The face on the bottom of a solid figure.

Example:

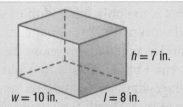

$h = 7$ in.

$w = 10$ in. $l = 8$ in.

rectangular solid

To find the surface area of a rectangular, square, or triangular solid figure, you *could* add up the areas of all its faces. There is an easier way to find the surface area of a rectangular solid. The formula is: $2lw + 2lh + 2wh$

The surface area of the solid above is $(2 \times 8 \times 7) + (2 \times 8 \times 10) + (2 \times 7 \times 10) = 112 + 160 + 140 = 412$ **square inches**

Exercises   CALCULATE SURFACE AREA

1

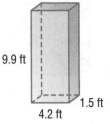

3 in.
3 in.
3 in.

_____

2

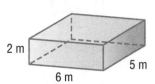

2 m
6 m
5 m

_____

3

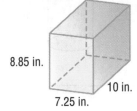

8.85 in.
10 in.
7.25 in.

_____

4

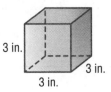

9.9 ft
1.5 ft
4.2 ft

_____

5

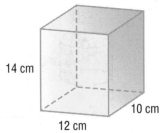

14 cm
10 cm
12 cm

_____

6

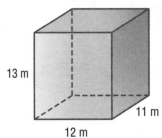

13 m
11 m
12 m

_____

7

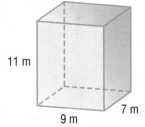

11 m
7 m
9 m

_____

8

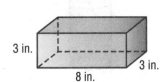

3 in.
3 in.
8 in.

_____

9

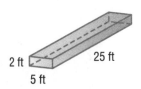

2 ft
25 ft
5 ft

_____

Surface Area of Solid Figures (cont.)

A **cylinder** is the only other kind of solid figure you will work with. To calculate the surface area of a cylinder, you *could* measure the area of each of its circular bases. Then you could unfold the rest of the cylinder to make a rectangle, and find the area of that. Finally, you could add the three surface areas you calculated.

Example:

There is an easier way to find the surface area of a cylinder. Use the formula: $2\pi r^2 + 2\pi rh$.

So the surface area of this cylinder
$= 2 \times \pi \times 3^2 + 2 \times \pi \times 3 \times 3$
$= 18\pi + 18\pi = 36\pi$ square centimeters.

Exercises **CALCULATE SURFACE AREA**

Keep your answer in the form of pi.

13

3 cm
7 cm

_____

14

5 in.
12 in.

_____

15

9 m
5 m

_____

16

11 m
1.5 m

_____

17

4.5 ft
6.2 ft

_____

18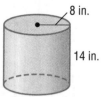

8 in.
14 in.

_____

19

6 cm
1 cm

_____

20

4.25 in.
12 in.

_____

21

10 in.
20 in.

_____

Volume of Solid Figures

You can calculate the volume of solid figures. The ones you will need to work with right now are rectangular solids, triangular solids, and cylinders.

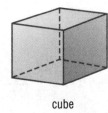
cube

You have already learned how to calculate the volume (V) of a rectangular solid.

$V = l \times w \times h$

The volume of a cylinder is the area of the circular base (B) × the height of the solid (h). The formula is $V = B \times h$.

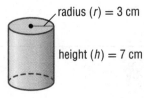
radius (r) = 3 cm
height (h) = 7 cm

$V = \pi r^2 \times h$
$= \pi \times 3^2 \times 7$
$= 63\pi$ cu cm

The volume of a triangular prism is the area of a triangular base (B) × the height of the solid (H). Remember that the area of the triangular base is $\frac{1}{2} \times l \times h$. The small letter h represents the height of a 2-dimensional *triangle*. The capital letter H represents the height of a 3-dimensional *solid*. Be careful, because they are usually different numbers. The formula for volume is $V = B \times H$.

9 ft (H)
3 ft (h)
4 ft (l)
Base

$V = \frac{1}{2} l \times h \times H$
$= \frac{1}{2} \times 4 \times 3 \times 9$
$= 54$ cu ft

Exercises   CALCULATE VOLUME

1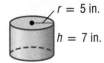
r = 5 in.
h = 7 in.

_____

2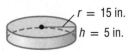
r = 15 in.
h = 5 in.

_____

3
h = 2 in.
l = 10 in.
w = 5 in.

_____

4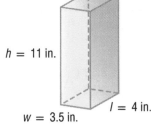
h = 11 in.
l = 4 in.
w = 3.5 in.

_____

5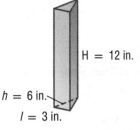
H = 12 in.
h = 6 in.
l = 3 in.

_____

6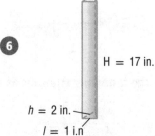
H = 17 in.
h = 2 in.
l = 1 i.n

_____

Name _____

Lessons 22–24

Identify each angle as obtuse, acute, or right.

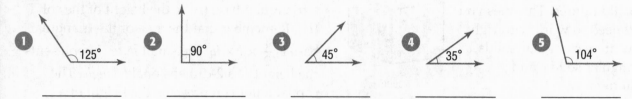

① 125° **②** 90° **③** 45° **④** 35° **⑤** 104°

_____ _____ _____ _____ _____

Identify each pair of angles as supplementary, complementary, vertical, or not any of these. Explain why.

⑥ _____

⑦ _____

⑧ _____

⑨ _____

⑩ _____

Identify the following triangles as scalene, equilateral, or isosceles.

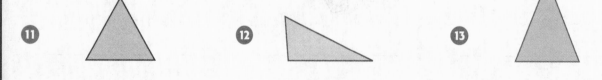

⑪ _____ **⑫** _____ **⑬** _____

Lessons 22–24

14  _____

15  _____

16 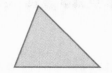 _____

Identify the following triangles as obtuse, right, or acute.

17  _____

18 _____

19 _____

20 _____

21 _____

22 _____

Answer the following questions by looking at the figure on the right.

23 Name the center point _____

24 Which segments are chords? _____

25 Which segment is the diameter? _____

26 Which segments are radii? _____

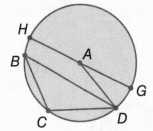

Identify the figures and fill in the missing information.

27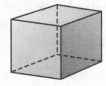

Figure _____
Base is _____
Number of faces _____
Number of edges _____
Number of vertices _____

28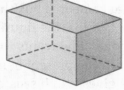

Figure _____
Base is _____
Number of faces _____
Number of edges _____
Number of vertices _____

29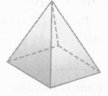

Figure _____
Base is _____
Number of faces _____
Number of edges _____
Number of vertices _____

30

Figure _____

Base is _____

Number of faces _____

Number of edges _____

Number of vertices _____

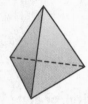

31

Figure _____

Base is _____

Number of faces _____

Number of edges _____

Number of vertices _____

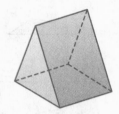

32

Figure _____

Base is _____

Number of faces _____

Number of edges _____

Number of vertices _____

Identify the figures.

33

_____

34

_____

35

_____

36

_____

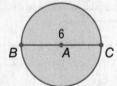

37

What is the circumference of the circle? (Use 3.14 for π).

_____

What is the area of the circle?

_____

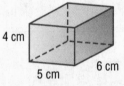

38

Jerome bought a present that came in a box that looked like the figure above. If he wants to wrap the present before he gives it to his sister, how much wrapping paper will he need to wrap the present?

_____

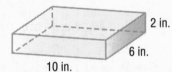

39

How many 1-inch cube wooden blocks can fit in the box shown in the figure?

_____

Complete the following test items on pages 137–140.

1 Restate the number 5,176,802.4539.

Expanded form: _____

Written form: _____

2 Brian's Bakery is having a sale on cakes. They have 95 cakes and will be baking 23 more before the start of the sale. If at the end of the sale they still have 7 cakes, how many cakes did they sell? _____

3 Stuart pedals 19 miles a day on his bicycle. How many miles does he pedal in the month of February? (Remember, February has 28 days.) _____

4 $\begin{array}{r} 134 \\ \times\ 15 \\ \hline \end{array}$ **5** $\begin{array}{r} 133 \\ \times\ 40 \\ \hline \end{array}$ **6** $\begin{array}{r} 432 \\ \times\ 51 \\ \hline \end{array}$ **7** $\begin{array}{r} 223 \\ \times\ 79 \\ \hline \end{array}$

8 $19\overline{)532}$ **9** $12\overline{)252}$ **10** $48\overline{)932}$ **11** $29\overline{)696}$

12 Danetta bought $19\frac{3}{8}$ kilograms of gerbil food. On the way home, she spilled $3\frac{4}{5}$ kilograms. How much gerbil food does she still have?

_____

13 To make his favorite fruit punch, Ezekiel mixes 1,950 centiliters of juice with $1\frac{4}{9}$ liters of seltzer and $\frac{3}{8}$ liters of orange juice. How many liters of punch will this make?

_____

14 $3\frac{7}{12} + 5\frac{1}{5} + \frac{1}{4} =$ _____   **15** $-5 + 17 - (-6) + 7(-5) - \frac{9}{3} =$ _____

16 Solve for x: $x - 91 = 13$ _____   **17** Solve for x: $4x + 11 = 15$ _____

18 What property is represented by the following equation?
$2(6 + 9) = 2 \times 6 + 2 \times 9$

_____

19 What property is represented by the following equation?
$(4 + 8) + 8 = 4 + (8 + 8)$

_____

20 $7 + (1 + 3)^2 - (9 \div 3) + 5(8 \times 3) + 2(10 - 7) =$

_____

21 Give the coordinates for the points.

A _____

B _____

C _____

D _____

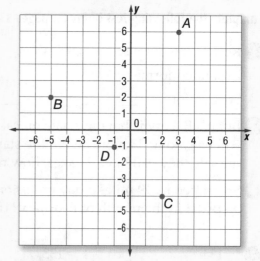

22 Restate in exponent form, then solve:

$5 \times 5 \times 5 + 3 \times 3 =$

_____

23 What is the area of the rectangle?

_____

What is the perimeter of the rectangle?

_____

18 cm

17 cm

24 What is the area of the circle? (Use 3.14 for π.)

_____

What is the circumference of the circle?

_____

B 9 cm C

25 Identify the following angles as obtuse, acute, or right.

95°

90°

45°

_____   _____   _____

26 Identify the triangles as scalene, isosceles, or equilateral.

_____   _____   _____

27 Jackie spends $37.95 a month on art supplies. She is working on a project that will take 19 months to finish. How much should she plan to spend on art supplies for the project? _____

28 Restate 7.6 as an improper fraction and a mixed number. _____

29 Restate $2\frac{3}{8}$ as a decimal. _____

30 Is the following true or false? $\frac{4}{11} = \frac{68}{187}$ _____

31 Put the following numbers in order from least to greatest:
1.141, 1.014, 1.044, 1.004, 1.9, 1.996, 1.89, .9

_____

32 Juliette deposits $295 in a bank account that earns 6% simple interest. How much money will she have in the account after 1 year?

_____ After 2 years? _____

33 What is the mode of the data distribution?

_____

What is the median?

_____

Stems	Leaves
1	4 6
2	2 7 5
3	1 6 6 6
4	3 3 5 7 7
5	2 5 6

34 $\frac{2}{7} \times 2\frac{5}{22} =$ _____

35 What is $\frac{5}{8}$ of 75%? _____

36 What is 25% of .525? _____

37 $.24\overline{)564}$

38 $\frac{5}{4} + \frac{7}{4} + \frac{15}{4} - \frac{9}{4} - \frac{17}{4} =$ _____

39 Identify each quadrilateral as a square, rectangle, kite, rhombus, or trapezoid.

_____   _____   _____   _____   _____

40 Identify the following figures.

_____   _____   _____

41 Restate $9\frac{11}{13}$ as an improper fraction.

_____

42 Restate $\frac{72}{13}$ as a mixed number.

_____

43 What are the chances of choosing a blue marble out of a bag containing 7 red marbles, 6 green marbles, 11 yellow marbles, and 4 blue marbles? _____

Name _____

44 According to the graph, how many miles did Janice swim in September?

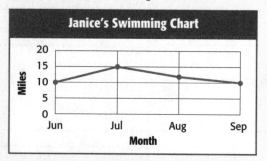

Janice's Swimming Chart

_____

45 During which week did Brian and Ray run the same distance?

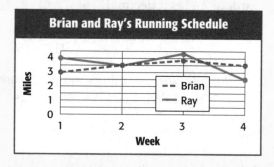

Brian and Ray's Running Schedule

_____

46 Which vegetable is most preferred by the students?

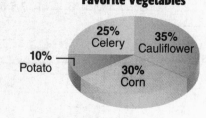

Favorite Vegetables

25% Celery
35% Cauliflower
10% Potato
30% Corn

_____

47 Dean's score was about 20 points higher than whose score?

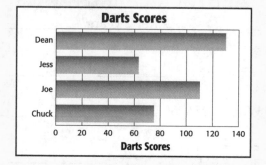

Darts Scores

_____

48 What is the range of the data in the box-and-whisker plot below?

_____

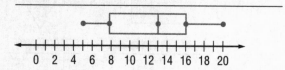

49 How much plastic wrap would you need to cover this rectangular solid?

_____

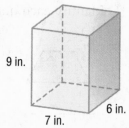

9 in.

6 in.

7 in.

50 Name two line segments. _____

Name 4 rays. _____

Name a line. _____

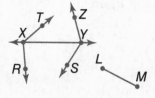

51 Fill in a Venn Diagram that displays the following data:
There are two groups of students, 25 who are in the drama club and 15 who enjoy math. There are 8 students who are in the drama club who also enjoy math.

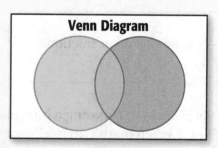

Venn Diagram

Glossary

Absolute Value: A number without its sign; it represents the distance between the number and 0 on the number line. *(p. 97)*

Acute Angle: An angle with a measure of less than 90°. *(p. 123)*

Acute Triangle: A triangle with only acute angles, angles less than 90°. *(p. 126)*

Addend: Any number that is added to another number. *(p. 10)*

Algebra: A branch of math used to find the value of unknown variables. *(p. 93)*

Algebraic Expression: A group of letters, numbers, and symbols used in a series of operations. *(p. 93)*

Angle: Two rays that share an endpoint. *(p. 123)*

Area: The measure of a 2- or 3-dimensional figure's interior, given in square units. *(p. 107)*

Associative Property of Addition: States that addends may be grouped in any order without changing the sum. *(p. 90)*

Associative Property of Multiplication: States that numbers may be grouped in any way without changing the product. *(p. 90)*

Bar Graph: A graph that uses numbers to compare two or more people, places, or things. Each bar represents a number and may be represented horizontally or vertically. *(p. 69)*

Base: The face on the bottom of a solid figure. *(p. 131)*

Base of an Exponent: The number being used as the factor when writing in exponential form. In the statement 10^3, the base is 10. *(p. 86)*

Box-and-Whisker Plot: Organizes data to show where the most data points lie and also shows the median of the data. *(p. 79)*

Carry: To place an extra digit—when adding or multiplying—in the next place-value column on the left. *(p. 10)*

Celsius: Used in the metric system to measure temperature and expressed as °C, also expressed as Centigrade. *(p. 115)*

Chord: A line segment with both endpoints on a circle's circumference. *(p. 129)*

Circle: A 2-dimensional figure with every point on its circumference an equal distance from its center point. *(p. 129)*

Circle Graph: Shows parts of a whole as a percentage to the whole and is also known as a pie chart. *(p. 75)*

Circumference: The length of distance around a circle's perimeter. *(p. 129)*

Coefficient: The number that replaces the symbol × and multiplies the variable in a multiplication expression. The statement $9m$ shows 9 as the coefficient and m as the variable. *(p. 93)*

Common Denominator: A number which can be divided evenly by all the denominators in a group of fractions. *(p. 26)*

Commutative Property of Additions: States that numbers may be added in any order without changing the sum. *(p. 90)*

Commutative Property of Multiplication: States that multiplication may be done in any order without changing the product. *(p. 90)*

Compatible Numbers: Numbers that are easy to work with in your head. *(p. 18)*

Complementary Angles: Two angles that form a right angle. Their sum is 90°. *(p. 124)*

Congruent: A term used to describe something that is equal. *(p. 126)*

Cross-multiplying: A method for finding a missing numerator or denominator. *(p. 38)*

Customary Units of Length: Measurements expressed in inches (in.), feet (ft), yards (yd), and miles (mi). *(p. 103)*

Customary Units of Weight: Measurements expressed in ounces (oz), pounds (lb), and tons. *(p. 105)*

Cylinder: A three-dimensional figure with two parallel and congruent circular bases and one curved surface. *(p. 132)*

Data: Information that is gathered and sometimes displayed in graphs and charts. *(p. 69)*

Denominator: The number below the line in a fraction. *(p. 22)*

Diameter: A chord that passes through a circle's center point. *(p. 129)*

Distributive Property of Multiplication: States that each number may be multiplied separately and added together. *(p. 91)*

Dividend: The number to be divided in a division problem. *(p. 16)*

Divisor: The number by which another number—the dividend—will be divided. *(p. 16)*

Double-Line Graph: Compares how information changes as time passes between two or more people, places, or things. *(p. 73)*

Edge: The line on a solid figure where two faces meet. *(p. 131)*

Equality Property of Addition: States that when adding a number on one side of an equation, you must add the same number on the other side of an equation. Both sides will then still be equal. *(p. 92)*

Equality Property of Division: States that when dividing a number on one side of an equation, you must divide by the *same* number on the other side of the equation. Both sides will still be equal. *(p. 92)*

Equality Property of Multiplication: States that when multiplying a number on one side of an equation, you must multiply by the *same* number on the other side of the equation. Both sides will still be equal. *(p. 92)*

Equality Property of Subtraction: States that when subtracting a number on one side of an equation, you must subtract the *same* number on the other side of the equation. Both sides will then still be equal. *(p. 92)*

Equation: A mathematical statement used to show that two amounts are equal. *(p. 38)*

Equilateral Triangle: A triangle with all three sides being the same length. *(p. 126)*

Exponent: The number that tells how many times the base number is multiplied by itself. The exponent ^{3} in 10^3 shows $10 \times 10 \times 10$. *(p. 86)*

Face: The flat surface of a solid figure. On a solid figure each face looks two-dimensional. *(p. 131)*

First Power: In an exponent, a base raised to the first power equals the base. *(p. 86)*

Identity Elements: Numbers in a problem that do not affect the answer. Only addition and multiplication have identity elements. *(p. 91)*

Improper Fraction: A fraction greater than 1 because its numerator is greater than its denominator. *(p. 22)*

Intersecting Lines: Lines that meet or cross each other at a specific point. *(p. 121)*

Interval: The distance between each measurement of time on a line graph. *(p. 121)*

Inverse: A number's exact opposite on the other side of the number line. The inverse of −9 is 9. *(p. 96)*

Isosceles Triangle: A triangle with two sides the same length, but the third side being a different length. *(p. 126)*

Kite: A quadrilateral with two angles that are equal, two touching sides that are equal in length, and the other two touching sides are equal in length. *(p. 127)*

Like Denominators: Fractions that have the same denominator. *(p. 24)*

Line: A straight path that goes in both directions and does not end. A line is measured in length. *(p. 121)*

Line Graph: Often used to show a change in information as time passes. The distance from one time to another is an interval. *(p. 71)*

Line Segment: A specific part of a line that ends at two identified points. *(p. 122)*

Liquid Volume: Units of liquid a container can hold and expressed in cups (c), pints (pt), quarts (qt), and gallons (gal). *(p. 104)*

Lower Extreme: The lowest number in a group of data used in a box-and-whisker plot. *(p. 79)*

Lower Quartile: The median of numbers from the lower extreme to the median on a box-and-whisker plot. *(p. 79)*

Glossary

Mean: The total number of the whole collection divided by the number of addends. (p. 77)

Median: The middle number in a set of numbers when the numbers are arranged from least to greatest. (p. 77)

Mixed Number: A number with a whole number part and a fraction part. (p. 22)

Metric Units of Length: Measurements expressed in millimeters (mm), centimeters (cm), meters (m), and kilometers (km). (p. 110)

Metric Units of Liquid Volume: Measurements expressed in liter (L), milliliters (mL), centiliters (cL), and kiloliters (kL). (p. 111)

Metric Units of Mass: Measurements expressed in grams (g), milligrams (mg), centigrams (cg), and kilograms (kg). (p. 112)

Mixed Number: A number with a whole number part and a fraction part. (p. 22)

Mode: The number that appears most often in a set of numbers. (p. 77)

Negative Exponent: A negative exponent creates a fraction. (p. 87)

Negative Number: A number less than 0 and identified with the minus sign. (p. 96)

Numerator: The number above the line in a fraction. (p. 22)

Obtuse Angle: An angle with a measure of more than 90°. (p. 123)

Obtuse Triangle: A triangle with one obtuse angle. (p. 126)

Order of Operations: Rules that tell the steps to follow when doing a computation. (p. 89)

Ordered Pair: Numbers used to identify a point on a grid. (p. 99)

Origin of a Circle: The circle's center point. (p. 129)

Percent: A special ratio that compares a number to 100 using the % symbol. (p. 60)

Perimeter: The distance around a figure. Measured in customary or metric units. (p. 106)

Periods: Organization of numbers in groups of three in a place-value chart. (p. 8)

Pi: The ratio of a circle's diameter to its circumference—a ratio that is exactly the same for every circle. A circle's circumference equals pi times its diameter. A circle's area equals *pi* times the square of its radius. *Pi* is often rounded to 3.14. (p. 130)

Place Value: The value of a position of a digit in a number. (p. 8)

Point: An exact location in space that has no dimensions and cannot be measured. A point is usually represented by a dot. (p. 121)

Polygon: Any closed two-dimensional figure that is made up of line segments. Triangles and quadrilaterals are two types of polygons. (p. 128)

Power of 10: In a place-value chart, each place value is 10 times the place value of the number to its right. (p. 52)

Principal: The amount borrowed or deposited into a bank. (p. 64)

Probability: The likelihood of an event happening in the future. (p. 82)

Product: The result, or answer, of a multiplication problem. (p. 13)

Property of Additive Inverse: States that when adding a negative number to its inverse the sum will be 0. For example: $-8 + 8 = 0$. (p. 96)

Proportion: An equation that shows two ratios are equal. (p. 38)

Quadrilateral: A two-dimensional figure with four sides and four angles. (p. 127)

Quotient: The result of dividing one number by another. (p. 16)

Radius: A line segment that starts at a circle's center point and extends to its perimeter. (p. 129)

Range: The greatest number minus the smallest number in a set of numbers. (p. 77)

Rate: A comparison of two different units or numbers. (p. 39)

Ratio: A comparison of two numbers using division. (p. 138)

Ray: A part of a line that extends from a specific point in only one direction. (p. 122)

Reciprocals: Two fractions that look like upside-down reflections of one another. (p. 31)

Rectangle: A quadrilateral with four right angles. A rectangle's opposite sides are parallel and the same length. (p. 127)

Reducing: The act of changing a fraction to its simplest form. (p. 32)

Regroup: In place value, to use part of the value from one place in another place to make adding or subtracting easier. (p. 10)

Remainder: The number left over in whole-number division when you can no longer divide any further. (p. 16)

Rhombus: A quadrilateral having four equal sides with opposite sides parallel. (p. 127)

Right Angle: An angle that measures exactly 90°. (p. 123)

Right Triangle: A triangle with one right angle, an angle with a measure of exactly 90°. (p. 126)

Rounding: To drop or zero-out digits in a number to a higher or lower value. (p. 12)

Rounding Place: The highest place value used in rounding. (p. 12)

Scalene Triangle: A triangle with all three sides being of different lengths. (p. 126)

Scientific Notation: A way of writing numbers as the product of a power of 10 and a decimal that is greater than 1 but less than 10. (p. 88)

Solid Figure: A three-dimensional figure such as a cube or pyramid. (p. 113, 131)

Square: A quadrilateral with four right angles and four sides that are the same length. (p. 127)

Statistics: A branch of math that answers questions about how many, how long, how often, how far, or how big. (p. 77)

Stem-and-Leaf Plot: Used to organize data and compare it. A stem-and-leaf plot organizes data from least to greatest using the digits or the greatest place value to group data. (p. 78)

Supplementary Angles: Any two angles that add up to a sum of 180°. (p. 124)

Tree Diagram: Used to show possible combinations of data including people, places, or things in a diagram that looks like a tree with branches. (p. 80)

Trapezoid: A quadrilateral that has two sides that are parallel to each other and two sides that are not parallel. (p. 127)

Triangle: A two-dimensional figure with three sides. (p. 126)

Upper Extreme: The highest number in a group of data used in a box-and-whisker plot. (p. 79)

Upper Quartile: The median of the numbers from the median to the upper extreme on a box-and-whisker plot. (p. 129)

Variable: An unknown number usually expressed as a letter and used in Algebra. In the statement n – 18, n is the variable. (p. 93)

Venn Diagram: A diagram used to show data and how different sets of data can overlap. (p. 81)

Vertex: The specific point of a ray, also called an endpoint. (p. 131)

Vertex of a Solid: A specific point at which more than two faces meet, or a point where a curve begins. (p. 131)

Vertical Angles: The angles opposite each other when two lines intersect. (p. 124)

Volume: The number of units a solid figure contains, expressed in cubic inches, feet, yards, or miles. (p. 108)

Whole Number: A number that does not include a fraction or decimal. (p. 10)

Zero Power: In an exponent, a base raised to the zero power equals 1. (p. 86)

Zero Property of Multiplication: States that any number times zero equals zero. (p. 92)

Answers

Lesson 1.1

1. Hundred thousands
2. Tenths
3. Thousands
4. Ones
5. Hundreds
6. 5
7. Tens
8. Ones
9. Hundredths
10. Hundredths
11. $(7 \times 1000) + (6 \times 100) + (4 \times 10) + (2 \times 1)$
12. Four million three hundred forty thousand two hundred
13. 326,523
14. 4,000,035
15. $(4 \times 100,000) + (3 \times 10,000) + (5 \times 1000) + (4 \times 100) + (1 \times 1)$
16. 79,302
17. $(7 \times 1,000,000,000) + (2 \times 100,000) + (1 \times 10,000) + (3 \times 1,000) + (3 \times 10) + (4 \times 1)$
18. 682,665
19. 3,431,400
20. $(6 \times 1,000,00) + (1 \times 100) + (1 \times 1)$

Lesson 1.2

1. 12
2. 110
3. 2121
4. 78
5. 1222
6. 99
7. 167
8. 550
9. 24
10. 898
11. 89
12. 692
13. 997,655
14. 98
15. 5,678
16. 9,310
17. 382
18. 955
19. 917
20. 3,649
21. 1,109
22. 421
23. 1,002
24. 610
25. 858
26. 82
27. 172
28. 180
29. 5,098
30. 1,889
31. 1,112
32. 1,332
33. 589
34. 13
35. 1,514
36. 2,876

Lesson 1.3

1. 200
2. 600
3. 100
4. 800
5. 160
6. 70
7. 250
8. 100
9. 1,200
10. 1,200
11. 500
12. 30
13. 52,000
14. 4,900
15. 700
16. 500
17. 90,000
18. 4,800
19. 4,000

Lesson 2.1

1. 60
2. 352
3. 133
4. 572
5. 861
6. 2,860
7. 1,641
8. 40,848
9. 2,376
10. 89,082
11. 3,599
12. 1,083
13. 612
14. 161,296
15. 3,762
16. 183,090
17. 76,445
18. 208,803
19. 1,519
20. 1,875
21. 625
22. 343
23. 7,225
24. 4,056
25. 68,820
26. 169
27. 1,323
28. 41,085
29. 36,663
30. 42,174
31. 100,899
32. 1,081
33. 2,250 potatoes
34. 1,320 stamps

Lesson 2.2

1. 2,100
2. 15,000
3. 3,500
4. 42,000
5. 32,000
6. 20,000
7. 150,000
8. 16,000
9. 2,500
10. 40,000
11. 560,000
12. 35,000
13. 60,000
14. 5,600
15. 300,000
16. 90,000
17. 350,000
18. 18,000
19. 16,000
20. 30,000

Lesson 3.1

1. 56 R3
2. 45 R5
3. 789 R7
4. 527 R8
5. 639 R10
6. 45 R20
7. 85 R1
8. 36 R9
9. 56 R4
10. 963 R4
11. 987 R10
12. 82 R7
13. 211 R8
14. 36 R9
15. 145 R15
16. 148 R11
17. 634 R4
18. 963 R9
19. 964 R5
20. 45 R4
21. 78 R19
22. 85 R2
23. 94 R5

Answers

24. 44 R32

25. 65 R12

26. 91 R5

27. 13 R10

28. 156 R72

29. 15 days

30. 50 people

Lesson 3.2

1. 60

2. 200

3. 80

4. 300

5. 3000

6. 500

7. 4000

8. 15

9. 20

10. 3000

11. 35

12. 200

13. 25

14. 300

15. 200

16. 70

17. 3200

18. 2000

19. 1800

20. 1300

Lesson 4.1

1. $14\frac{2}{3}$

2. $22\frac{3}{4}$

3. $2\frac{1}{2}$

4. $7\frac{1}{3}$

5. $4\frac{7}{12}$

6. $9\frac{8}{11}$

7. $9\frac{3}{4}$

8. $3\frac{7}{8}$

9. $4\frac{17}{21}$

10. $16\frac{1}{2}$

11. $4\frac{3}{11}$

12. $10\frac{12}{19}$

13. $9\frac{3}{4}$

14. $6\frac{5}{7}$

15. $12\frac{1}{4}$

16. $16\frac{1}{4}$

17. $19\frac{1}{3}$

18. $19\frac{1}{4}$

19. $11\frac{1}{12}$

20. $49\frac{2}{7}$

Lesson 4.2

1. $\frac{13}{4}$

2. $\frac{38}{7}$

3. $\frac{135}{11}$

4. $\frac{73}{5}$

5. $\frac{15}{13}$

6. $\frac{297}{14}$

7. $\frac{298}{9}$

8. $\frac{69}{17}$

9. $\frac{715}{7}$

10. $\frac{65}{2}$

11. $\frac{842}{29}$

12. $\frac{299}{8}$

13. $\frac{47}{3}$

14. $\frac{859}{14}$

15. $\frac{121}{17}$

16. $\frac{135}{22}$

17. $\frac{71}{3}$

18. $\frac{109}{7}$

19. $\frac{170}{13}$

20. $\frac{180}{44}$

Lesson 4.3

1. 1

2. $\frac{7}{5}$

3. $\frac{10}{8} = \frac{5}{4}$

4. $\frac{8}{7}$

5. $\frac{24}{11}$

6. $\frac{74}{17}$

7. $\frac{38}{9}$

8. $\frac{9}{3} = 3$

9. $\frac{58}{23}$

10. $\frac{57}{37}$

11. $\frac{8}{4} = 2$

12. $\frac{12}{11}$

13. $\frac{15}{27}$

14. $\frac{16}{4} = 4$

15. $\frac{42}{24} = \frac{7}{4}$

16. $\frac{13}{37}$

Lesson 4.4

1. $\frac{2}{4} = \frac{1}{2}$

2. $\frac{2}{8} = \frac{1}{4}$

3. $\frac{6}{4} = \frac{3}{2}$

4. $\frac{6}{5}$

5. $\frac{4}{7}$

6. $\frac{2}{11}$

7. $\frac{7}{3}$

8. $\frac{8}{19}$

9. 2

10. $\frac{6}{7}$

11. $\frac{8}{8} = 1$

12. $\frac{8}{51}$

13. $\frac{29}{13}$

14. $\frac{21}{17}$

15. $\frac{4}{4} = 1$

16. $\frac{18}{37}$

Lesson 4.5

1. $\frac{9}{20}$

2. $\frac{20}{21}$

3. $\frac{83}{60}$

4. $\frac{11}{26}$

5. $\frac{17}{28}$

6. $\frac{136}{105}$

7. $\frac{74}{33}$

8. $\frac{50}{21}$

9. $\frac{3}{15} = \frac{1}{5}$

10. $\frac{19}{40}$

11. $\frac{400}{7}$

12. $\frac{17}{60}$

13. $\frac{142}{39}$

14. $\frac{7}{20}$

15. $\frac{11}{4}$

Lesson 4.6

1. $5\frac{3}{4}$

2. $8\frac{2}{21}$

3. $12\frac{7}{12}$

4. $6\frac{1}{12}$

5. $13\frac{7}{10}$

6. $69\frac{1}{6}$

7. $23\frac{8}{21}$

8. $7\frac{32}{63}$

9. $18\frac{4}{55}$

10. $80\frac{31}{78}$

11. $36\frac{37}{55}$

12. $8\frac{1}{21}$

13. $12\frac{23}{60}$

14. $457\frac{61}{66}$

15. $145\frac{29}{42}$

16. $143\frac{7}{8}$

Lesson 4.7

1. $3\frac{1}{4}$

2. $6\frac{19}{77}$

3. $17\frac{7}{45}$

4. $3\frac{11}{18}$

5. $9\frac{1}{2}$

6. $10\frac{7}{36}$

7. $10\frac{29}{42}$

8. $14\frac{29}{55}$

9. $6\frac{1}{22}$

10. $2\frac{1}{9}$

11. $36\frac{28}{51}$

12. $16\frac{9}{14}$

13. $\frac{3}{4}$ hours

14. No

Lessons 4.8

1. 37

2. 93

3. 111

4. 168

5. 5045

6. 359

7. 121

8. 512

9. 504

10. 101

11. $114\frac{1}{2}$

12. $311\frac{1}{2}$

13. 25 ounces

14. About $8\frac{1}{2}$ dozen cookies

Lesson 5.1

1. $\frac{3}{4}$

2. $\frac{30}{7} = 4\frac{2}{7}$

3. $4\frac{1}{2}$

4. 6

5. $2\frac{1}{4}$

6. $3\frac{11}{17}$

7. $1\frac{3}{4}$

8. $12\frac{8}{11}$

9. $2\frac{2}{9}$

10. $4\frac{2}{3}$

11. $9\frac{3}{5}$

12. $10\frac{1}{12}$

13. 30

14. $1\frac{1}{2}$

15. 20

16. 1

17. 3

18. 1

19. 39

20. 4

Lesson 5.2

1. $\frac{1}{3}$

2. $\frac{15}{56}$

3. $\frac{8}{21}$

4. $\frac{9}{4}$

5. 1

6. $\frac{28}{3}$

7. 5

8. $\frac{3}{49}$

9. 1

10. 18

11. $\frac{3}{52}$

12. $\frac{14}{3}$

13. $\frac{9}{7}$

14. $\frac{1}{2}$

15. $\frac{9}{16}$

16. $\frac{40}{7}$

Lesson 5.3

1. $2\frac{5}{8}$

2. $1\frac{7}{9}$

3. $18\frac{3}{8}$

4. $14\frac{2}{3}$

5. $\frac{7}{20}$

6. $4\frac{10}{21}$

7. $1\frac{13}{20}$

8. $2\frac{1}{32}$

9. $1\frac{8}{9}$

10. $1\frac{1}{12}$

11. $4\frac{5}{7}$

12. $9\frac{3}{10}$

13. $17\frac{1}{2}$

14. 12

15. $12\frac{3}{8}$

16. 12

Lesson 6 .1

1. $\frac{1}{8}$

2. $\frac{3}{20}$

3. $\frac{2}{7}$

4. $\frac{1}{55}$

5. $\frac{5}{38}$

6. $\frac{4}{35}$

7. $\frac{1}{81}$

8. $\frac{1}{44}$

9. $\frac{17}{72}$

10. $\frac{4}{13}$

11. $\frac{1}{9}$

12. $\frac{1}{44}$

13. $\frac{3}{77}$

14. $\frac{1}{27}$

15. $\frac{2}{11}$

16. $\frac{5}{26}$

17. $\frac{1}{5}$

18. $\frac{12}{65}$

19. $\frac{1}{22}$

20. $\frac{3}{28}$

Lesson 6.2

1. 20

2. $3\frac{3}{4}$

3. 49

4. $15\frac{3}{4}$

5. 4

6. 14

7. 21

8. 18

9. $25\frac{1}{2}$

Answers

10. $8\frac{1}{3}$

11. 9

12. $13\frac{1}{2}$

13. 55

14. 4

15. 27

16. $\frac{6}{7}$

Lesson 6.3

1. $\frac{20}{21}$

2. $2\frac{1}{3}$

3. $\frac{7}{27}$

4. $6\frac{3}{4}$

5. $1\frac{1}{26}$

6. $\frac{1}{3}$

7. $\frac{10}{13}$

8. $1\frac{1}{2}$

9. $5\frac{1}{3}$

10. $2\frac{13}{16}$

11. 6

12. $\frac{3}{4}$

13. $\frac{3}{242}$

14. 9

15. $2\frac{1}{2}$

16. $\frac{9}{32}$

Lesson 6.4

1. $\frac{8}{15}$

2. $3\frac{1}{5}$

3. $2\frac{1}{7}$

4. $1\frac{41}{84}$

5. 2

6. $1\frac{7}{15}$

7. $1\frac{8}{11}$

8. $3\frac{5}{7}$

9. $2\frac{1}{136}$

10. $1\frac{129}{143}$

11. $\frac{35}{92}$

12. $7\frac{1}{2}$

13. $9\frac{43}{45}$

14. $\frac{3}{7}$

15. $4\frac{1}{5}$

16. $\frac{39}{110}$

Lesson 7.1

1. 2:1 or $\frac{2}{1}$

2. 3:2 or $\frac{3}{2}$

3. 25:18 or $\frac{25}{18}$

4. $\frac{32}{17}$ or 32:17

5. $\frac{4}{3}$ or 4:3

Lesson 7.2

1. $x = 10$

2. $z = 12$

3. $z = 7$

4. $y = 280$

5. $w = 15$

6. $x = 2$

7. $r = 9$

8. $z = 3$

9. $x = 7.5$

10. $w = 2.5$

11. $x = 54$

12. $q = 28$

Lesson 7.3

1. 80 cm

2. $12\frac{4}{5}$ teaspoons

3. 6

4. 5

Lesson 8.1

1. 46

2. 77

3. 146

4. 1001

5. 89

6. 1501

7. 14.4

8. 125.5

9. 149.5

10. 33.4

11. 275.8

12. 213

13. 1435.34

14. 3.56

15. 111.12

16. 32.76

17. 999.99

18. 954.38

19. 3.238

20. 329.330

21. 109.109

22. 8256.784

23. 49.495

24. .114

Lesson 8.2

1. .3125

2. .5714

3. .4839

4. .6000

5. .0236

6. .9394

7. .2866

8. .9231

9. .0005

10. .3026

11. .0938

12. .8333

13. .2553

14. .8750

15. .8667

16. .7647

Lesson 8.3

1. $\frac{17}{20}$

2. $\frac{77}{100}$

3. $\frac{111}{125}$

4. $\frac{1}{80}$

5. $\frac{339}{500}$

6. $\frac{1251}{2000}$

7. $\frac{331}{1000}$

8. $\frac{209}{2000}$

9. $\frac{219}{250}$

10. $\frac{5}{16}$

11. $\frac{687}{2000}$

12. $\frac{7007}{10000}$

13. $\frac{42}{125}$

14. $\frac{2141}{10000}$

15. $\frac{14}{25}$

16. $\frac{11}{2000}$

Lesson 8.4

1. 4

2. 10.10

3. .5677

4. 45.449

5. 14.00126

6. 21.21

7. 11.111

8. 12.1023

9. 166.66

10. 144.32

11. 25.205

12. 156.12

Answers

Lesson 9.1
1. 47.55
2. 74.92
3. 13.94
4. 5.221
5. 33.056
6. 22.3351
7. 6.382
8. 456.431
9. 14.0001
10. 68.56
11. 9.60201
12. 26.7041
13. 10.11
14. 65.1822
15. 152.15372
16. 5.5051
17. 11.613
18. 11.1102
19. 482.6242
20. 22.3801

Lesson 9.2
1. 7.63
2. 42.381
3. 85.91
4. 47.7015
5. 5.523
6. 94.737
7. 552.657
8. .707
9. .9414
10. 6.957
11. 26.07
12. .5738
13. 4233.77
14. 1.671
15. 11.871
16. 954.951
17. 6.999
18. 1.629
19. 4.07
20. 5.975

Lesson 9.3
1. $88.00
2. $27.91
3. $2.60
4. $11.38
5. $2.79
6. $17.71
7. $85.95
8. $29.23
9. $911.61
10. $47.30
11. $32.19
12. $805.29
13. $2.07
14. $67.89
15. $5.94
16. $1.21
17. $1473.13
18. $1510.93
19. $58.43
20. $38.60

Lesson 9.4
1. $57
2. $78
3. $79
4. $870
5. $11
6. $559
7. $22
8. $12
9. $144
10. $9
11. $15
12. $233
13. $4
14. $0.50
15. $512
16. $1234
17. $322
18. $83
19. $2527
20. $20

Lesson 10.1
1. 16.25
2. 15.048
3. 28.5212
4. 5367.24
5. .90012
6. 10.1101
7. 2088.1447
8. 425.606
9. .147852
10. 427.68
11. 2223.144
12. 2314.1
13. 61.84937
14. 199.4882
15. .00001274
16. 19.55

Lesson 10.1 (cont.)
1. .46731
2. 7135
3. 580
4. 1.645
5. .10005
6. 1112
7. 5.93
8. .00322
9. 105.632
10. 28.90
11. .156
12. 21000
13. 583.1
14. 8181
15. 9.73
16. .000002

Lesson 10.2
1. $18.08
2. $808.50
3. $76.95
4. $16.86
5. $15.44
6. $0.84
7. $506.68
8. $127.62
9. $1151.55
10. $485.22
11. $148.04
12. $164.01
13. $0.99
14. $152.20
15. $563.63
16. $22.15

Lesson 10.3
1. 150
2. 22
3. 1,100
4. 14
5. 1260
6. 3000
7. 3.5
8. 25
9. 160
10. 100
11. 50
12. 160
13. 13
14. 4
15. 3

Lesson 11.1
1. 9.14
2. 7.335
3. 7.1727
4. 5.9714
5. 1.15
6. 152.0667
7. 4.7571
8. 14.89
9. 53.2286
10. 5.9857
11. 1.2533
12. 8.9313
13. 240.875
14. 7.2333
15. 19.29
16. 9.5347

Answers

Lesson 11.2

1. 2.0833
2. .6593
3. 8.7302
4. 28.3117
5. 10.9090
6. 7.3333
7. 5.7746
8. 1.8182
9. 8.0899
10. 175.6000
11. 70.1639
12. 8.0882
13. 5.5102
14. 8.9109
15. 16.0000
16. 16.1818

Lesson 11.3

1. 2.4889
2. 2.2800
3. 10.9012
4. 2.1429
5. .7589
6. 7.3391
7. 3.7217
8. 2.3042
9. 1.3490
10. 3.0995
11. 2.5359
12. 1.1604
13. 3.0033
14. 470.0476
15. 2.3962
16. 23.2571

Lesson 11.4

1. 5
2. 11.2
3. 27.38
4. $4.35
5. $0.77
6. 5.61
7. $37.57

8. 5.15
9. $8.26
10. 2.15
11. 13.65
12. $960.80
13. 17.41
14. 6.93
15. $13.18
16. $2.17

Lesson 11.5

1. 100
2. 5
3. 1.5
4. 40
5. 300
6. .022
7. 21
8. 22
9. 3
10. 5
11. 7
12. 25
13. 20
14. 24
15. 7
16. 10
17. 20

Lesson 12.1

1. .07; $\frac{7}{100}$
2. .16; $\frac{4}{25}$
3. 1.00; $\frac{1}{1}$
4. .25; $\frac{1}{4}$
5. .01; $\frac{1}{100}$
6. .2; $\frac{1}{5}$
7. .44; $\frac{11}{25}$
8. .99; $\frac{99}{100}$
9. .23; $\frac{23}{100}$
10. .03; $\frac{3}{100}$
11. .0; $\frac{0}{100}$

12. .71; $\frac{71}{100}$
13. 89%
14. $\frac{1}{10}$
15. .10

Lesson 12.2

1. 50%
2. 15%
3. 46.7%; not simple %
4. 30%
5. 66.6%; not simple %
6. 75%
7. 54.5%; not simple %
8. 100%
9. 3.1%; not simple %
10. 16%
11. 38%
12. 6%
13. 140%
14. 55%
15. 12%
16. 44.4%; not simple %
17. 35%
18. 20000%

Lesson 12.3

1. .07
2. .185
3. 33%
4. 67.5%
5. 33.56%
6. .0001
7. .0234
8. 345%
9. 214.5%
10. .003
11. .3329
12. 245600%
13. 85.71%
14. $15.43

Lesson 12.4

1. 20%
2. 40%
3. 9

4. 48
5. 2%
6. 15
7. 117
8. 5%
9. 30%
10. 15
11. 9%
12. 9
13. 42
14. 37
15. 9%

Lesson 12.5

1. $175.00
2. $216.00
3. $6.00
4. $465.75
5. $350.00
6. $100.00
7. $4200.00
8. $16.50

Lesson 12.6

1. $625.00
2. $588.00
3. $2,786.62
4. $2,854.82
5. $35,256.00
6. $417.54

Lesson 13.1

1. Soft Boiled
2. Birds and Hamsters
3. Word Meaning
4. Juan
5. 0–3 Years
6. A and D
7. About 45% of the students improved their performances
8. It is getting warmer from 2000–2003

Answers

Lesson 13.2

1. Yes, there seems to be a steady increase in visitors with no seasonal ups and downs
2. Northern Hemisphere
3. Month 2 and Month 9
4. No
5. 1800–1810
6. 60 million
7. Good. It got warm by day 6.
8. 46

Lesson 13.3

1. The higher the sales, the higher the profits.
2. No. There is a big spike increase in salary with a corresponding decrease in happiness.
3. Males and Females are both living longer.
4. Expenditures are going up. Police are going up faster than the other two areas.

Lesson 13.4

1. No. Non-instruction is only 4% of the total.
2. No. He is more likely to pick blue, green, or red.
3. The manager would need the most employees in January and the fewest in February.
4. Romance and Comedy, or Romance and Sci-fi will equal 50% of the total.
5. 75%. Subtract the percentages that we know from 100%.
6. No. Cutting tools only account for 3% of the total.

7. 91%
8. No. The largest category is Apple at 36%, which is not more than 50%.

Lesson 14.1

1. 2.7
2. 5
3. 65
4. 3
5. 5
6. 9
7. 15.29
8. 12
9. 23.5
10. 12 and 13

Lesson 14.2

1. 80
2. 10, 17, 19, 21, 21, 23, 24, 26, 27, 28, 30, 31, 33, 35, 36, 37, 37, 40, 41, 41, 41, 42, 69
3. 80, 85, 71, 75, 76, 51, 56, 58, 40, 46
4. 45

Lesson 14.3

1. Botany, Zoology
2. Zoology
3. Range = 40; Median = 35

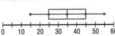

4. Lower quartile 15–25; Upper quartile 45–55

Lesson 14.4

1. 4; Red and Green −2
2.

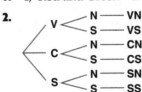

Lesson 14.5

1. Numbers that are even and divisible by b.
2.

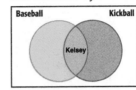

Lesson 14.6

1. $\frac{4}{12} = \frac{1}{3}$
2. $\frac{4}{52} = \frac{1}{13}$
3. $\frac{2}{4} = \frac{1}{2}$
4. $\frac{1}{5}$
5. $\frac{3}{14}$
6. $\frac{9}{35}$

Lesson 15.1

1. 144
2. 10000
3. 343
4. 8
5. 256
6. 125
7. 1681
8. 3125
9. 279,936
10. 83,521
11. 0
12. 1
13. 12
14. 1
15. 33

Lesson 15.1 (cont.)

1. 2^8
2. $\frac{1}{5}$
3. 11^7
4. 54^6
5. $3^2 = 9$
6. 8^9

7. $15^1 = 15$
8. 8^4
9. 18^{28}
10. 81^3
11. 19^{35}
12. $\frac{1}{21}$
13. $\frac{1}{15^{11}}$
14. $10^4 = 10000$
15. $\frac{1}{17^7}$

Lesson 15.3

1. 500,000
2. 4.7823×10^2
3. 8.9786×10^4
4. 6,721,000
5. .029731
6. 6.91273×10^5
7. .0059178
8. 87,234,500,000
9. 6.664475×10^6
10. 5.123×10^4
11. 8.9×10^0
12. 1.00235×10^2
13. 9.63764×10^5
14. 4.6554×10^0
15. 7.8923×10^2
16. 1.5896×10^{13}
17. 8.999345×10^9
18. 16,973.24

Lesson 16.1

1. 10
2. 4
3. 15
4. 12
5. 1
6. 6
7. 3
8. 21
9. 62
10. 12
11. 4
12. 48

Answers

Lesson 16.2

1. Commutative Property of Multiplication
2. Commutative Property of Addition
3. Associative Property of Multiplication
4. Commutative Property of Multiplication
5. Commutative Property of Multiplication
6. Associative Property of Multiplication
7. Commutative Property of Addition
8. Commutative Property of Multiplication
9. Associative Property of Addition
10. Commutative Property of Multiplication
11. Associative Property of Addition
12. Commutative Property of Multiplication

Lesson 16.3

1. 6
2. 28
3. 7
4. 36
5. 150
6. 30
7. 30
8. 48
9. 41
10. 175
11. 14
12. 110
13. 72
14. 0
15. 16

Lesson 16.4

1. 0
2. 0
3. 0
4. 35
5. 0
6. 0
7. 0
8. 2
9. 0
10. Yes. Equality Property of Multiplication
11. Yes. Equality Property of Addition
12. Yes. Equality Property of Subtraction
13. Yes. Equality Property of Division

Lesson 17.1

1. A number divided by four.
2. A number plus three.
3. Four times a number plus eight.
4. Nine-tenths of a number minus seven.
5. A number less three divided by twenty-five.
6. Eight times the sum of two times a number plus six.
7. Two times a number minus five.
8. Twelve times a number minus fourteen.
9. Seven divided by a number.
10. The sum of eleven plus a number divided by sixteen.

Lesson 17.2

1. $x = 11$
2. $s = 8$
3. $z = 35$
4. $f = 3$
5. $c = 22$
6. $y = 2$
7. $102 = l$
8. $k = 28$
9. $u = 28$
10. $37 = t$
11. $6 = a$
12. $b = 26$
13. $25 = e$
14. $d = 23$
15. $w = 66$
16. $q = 58$

Lesson 17.3

1. $y = 5$
2. $p = 13$
3. $c = 27$
4. $w = 84$
5. $6 = q$
6. $175 = z$
7. $28 = x$
8. $15 = g$
9. $108 = g$
10. $k = 17$
11. $195 = p$
12. $y = 34.5$
13. $d = 10$
14. $c = 99$

Lesson 18.1

1. 0
2. 100
3. 0
4. 20
5. 10
6. 0
7. 0
8. −200
9. −33
10. 6

Lesson 18.2

1. 14
2. −9
3. −11
4. 39
5. 68
6. 29
7. −33
8. 38
9. 8
10. 18
11. −11
12. 22
13. 28
14. 31
15. −2
16. 1

Lesson 18.3

1. −15
2. −130
3. −100
4. −69
5. −225
6. −240
7. 8
8. −1
9. 125
10. −309
11. −1
12. 0
13. 3
14. −3
15. −5
16. $\frac{1}{3}$

Lesson 18.4

1. (2,3)
2. (4,−4)
3. (−6,−6)
4. (5,3)
5. (3,5)
6. (1,2)

7. (−2,2)

8. (−5,4)

9. (9,7)

10. (−6,8)

11.

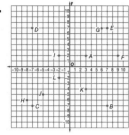

Lesson 19.1

1. $4\frac{1}{6}$ yd

2. 5280 ft

3. 4 yd

4. 5280 yd

5. $10\frac{2}{3}$ ft

6. 6 miles

7. 46.5 ft

8. 205,920 in.

9. 1134 in.

10. 44,000 yd

11. 8.1 miles

12. 624 in.

13. 1035 ft

14. 1 mile

15. $\frac{1}{2}$ mile

16. 252,000 in.

17. 530 yd

18. 880,000 yd

Lesson 19.2

1. 32 pints

2. 132 quarts

3. 16 gallons

4. $4\frac{1}{2}$ gallons

5. 500 quarts

6. 600 cups

7. 512 pints

8. 168 cups

9. 8 gallons

10. 66 quarts

11. 125 pints

12. 350 cups

13. 352 quarts

14. $5\frac{1}{4}$ gallons

15. 96 gallons

16. 112.5 pints

Lesson 19.3

1. 320 oz

2. 10400 lb

3. 128,000 oz

4. $12\frac{1}{4}$ lb

5. 7000 lb

6. .8 tons

7. 48000 oz

8. 42.5 lb

9. 6400 lb

10. 1.5 tons

11. 1043.2 oz

12. 2.5 tons

13. .3 tons

14. 27,000 lb

15. 3500 lb

16. $196\frac{7}{8}$ lb

Lesson 19.4

1. The hexagon has a perimeter of 108 ft.

2. 30 feet to get back, he walked 110 ft in total

3. 30 ft

4. 30 inches

5. 72 ft

Lesson 19.5

1. 6667 people

2. 312.5 sq ft

3. 84 sq ft

4. The square has an area of 196 sq ft, the triangle has an area of 187.5 sq ft

Lesson 19.6

1. 1,000 cu in.

2. $\frac{1}{3}$ cu ft

3. 585 cu ft

4. 37 cu yd

5. $13\frac{1}{3}$ lb of sugar

6. 7560 cu yd

Lesson 19.7

1. 129,600 seconds

2. 600 hours

3. 50400 minutes

4. 4 days

5. 46080 minutes

6. $2\frac{1}{12}$ hours

7. 13 weeks

8. 30 decades

9. 25 centuries

10. .01 weeks

11. $\frac{\$27.35}{hour}$

12. 259,200 widgets

13. 3

14. $720.00

Lesson 20.1

1. 3.35 m

2. 6.235 m

3. 576,100 cm

4. 725,020,000 mm

5. 3.9 m

6. 261,100 cm

7. .132 m

8. 6,872 mm

9. 8,065 m

10. 32,041,500 cm

11. 12.3932 m

12. .0054 km

13. 4535 cm

14. 76,355 mm

15. 1175.5 m

16. 67.3326 m

17. 2.104 km

18. .01545 km

Lesson 20.2

1. 2100 mL

2. 1.7 kL

3. 3456 mL

4. 350,000 mL

5. 3,901,000 mL

6. .16134 L

7. .000767 kL

8. 488.276 L

9. 2135 L

10. .141071 kL

11. 839.5 kL

12. 567.213 kL

13. 424.85532 L

14. 141256.8 mL

15. $26\frac{2}{3}$ bottles

16. 2,000,000 kL

17. 37.5 L

18. 240 cups

Lesson 20.3

1. .2 kg

2. 125,000,000 mg

3. .66 kg

4. 4.5 g

5. 11,300,000 mg

6. .3 g

7. 500.6 g

8. 719,000 cg

9. 2058 g

10. 266.867 kg

11. 353.654 g

12. 4.3033 kg

13. 5297.57 g

14. 14,000 g

15. 5.004002 kg

16. 300,303,000 mg

17. 14225.8 cg

18. 6.565 kg

Answers

Lesson 20.4

1. Perimeter: 28 cm
   Area: 49 sq cm
2. 8 mm
3. 216 cu cm, 216 sq cm
4. Perimeter 20.8 cm; 19.2 sq cm
5. Perimeter: 40 m
   Area: 70 sq cm
6. 8 times around the course
7. $88.80;
   perimeter 11.4 meters
8. 900 cu cm
9. 35 sq m
10. 240 cu m
11. 96 sq m
12. 192 sq mm

Lesson 20.5

1. 392° F
2. 55.6° C
3. 27.2° C
4. 89.6° F
5. 101.1° C
6. 160° C
7. −12.2° C
8. 113° F
9. 23.9° C
10. 194° F
11. −26.1° C
12. 54.4° C
13. 98.6° F
14. 3632° F
15. 471.2° F
16. 102.2° F
17. 176.7° C

Lesson 21.1

1. 7264 kg
2. 1360.8 g
3. 1814.36 kg
4. 87.055 L
5. .7095 L

6. Yes. The rope is 45.7 m long
7. 1.362 kg
8. 2.4 pounds of gold
9. 30.5 m
10. 2.9 m

Lesson 21.2

1. 20.8 gallons
2. 27.8 lb
3. 388.1 oz
4. 9.84 ft
5. 49.2 ft
6. 48.5 lb
7. 164.04 ft
8. 2,961,000,000 gallons
9. 3.726 miles
10. 2608.2 miles per hour
11. 118.2 inches; 9.9 ft
12. The offensive linemen have a lower average weight by 2.55 lb

Lesson 22.1

1. A, B, C, D
2. 8 points
3. No. A line must stretch infinitely in both directions
4. $\overrightarrow{ZX}$, $\overrightarrow{XZ}$, $\overrightarrow{ZY}$, $\overrightarrow{YZ}$, $\overrightarrow{YX}$, $\overrightarrow{XY}$

Lesson 22.2

1. 14 line segments
2. $\overrightarrow{BA}$
3. $\overline{BO}$, $\overline{OD}$, $\overline{BD}$, $\overline{AB}$,
   $\overline{AO}$, $\overline{OC}$, $\overline{CB}$, $\overline{BC}$,
   $\overline{OB}$, $\overline{DO}$, $\overline{DB}$, $\overline{BA}$,
   $\overline{OA}$, $\overline{CO}$
4. Ray 33–15, Ray 24–8, Ray 8–24, Ray 15–33

Lesson 23.1

1. Acute
2. Obtuse

3. Right
4. Acute
5. Obtuse
6. Acute
7. Right
8. Obtuse
9. Obtuse
10. Acute
11. Acute
12. Obtuse

Lesson 23.2

1. 50°
2. 103°
3. Angle T & angle V, angle T & angle S, angle S & angle X, angle X & angle V
4. F = 120°, E = 60°, H = 120°

Lesson 23.2 (cont.)

1. Complementary:
   ∠BGC and ∠BGA,
   ∠FGE and ∠DGE
   Supplementary:
   ∠BCG and ∠BGF,
   ∠AGC and ∠AGF,
   ∠BGA and ∠AGE
   Vertical: ∠BGC and ∠FGE, ∠DGC and ∠AGF, ∠AGB and ∠DGE
2. Complementary:
   ∠DFE and ∠CFD,
   ∠CFB and ∠AFB
   Supplementary:
   ∠AFB and ∠EFB,
   ∠AFC and ∠CFE,
   ∠DFE and ∠DFA
3. Yes, they form a right triangle.
4. COD = 50°
   COF = 90°
   FOY = 40°
   YOX = 50°
   FOX = 90°

Lesson 24.1

1. Acute
2. Obtuse
3. Right
4. Right
5. Acute
6. Obtuse
7. Isosceles
8. Equilateral
9. Scalene

Lesson 24.2

1. Square
2. Kite
3. Rectangle
4. Rhombus
5. Kite
6. Rhombus
7. Trapezoid
8. Rectangle
9. Square

Lesson 24.3

1. Hepatagon
2. Octagon
3. Pentagon
4. Hexagon
5. Hexagon
6. Octagon
7. Heptagon
8. Pentagon
9. Yes. Sides and angle measures are the same
10. No. The bases are of different lengths

Lesson 24.4

1. 5
2. 5 cm
3. $\overline{AX}$, $\overline{XB}$ radii, $\overline{AB}$ chord
4. $\overline{VY}$ radius, $\overline{WX}$ chord
5. $\overline{WX}$, $\overline{XY}$, $\overline{YZ}$, $\overline{ZV}$, $\overline{VW}$

Answers

6. No. $\overline{CD}$ does not go through center point O

7. $\overline{EA}$, $\overline{AE}$, $\overline{EC}$, $\overline{BE}$, $\overline{EB}$, $\overline{EC}$, $\overline{CE}$

8. $\overline{AB}$, $\overline{CD}$

9. $\overline{AQ}$ chord; $\overline{RA}$ diameter

10. 100π sq in.

11. Circumference 10π sq units; Area = 25π sq units

12. Circumference 14π sq units; Area = 49π sq units

Lesson 24.5

1. SA = 54 sq in.
2. SA = 104 sq m
3. SA = 450.325 sq in.
4. SA = 125.46 sq ft
5. SA = 856 sq cm
6. SA = 862 sq m
7. SA = 478 sq m
8. SA = 114 sq in.
9. SA = 370 sq ft
10. SA = 60π sq cm
11. SA = 170π sq in.
12. SA = 252π sq m
13. SA = 275π sq m
14. SA = 96.3π sq ft
15. SA = 352π sq in.
16. SA = 84π sq cm
17. SA = 138.125π sq in.
18. SA = 600π sq in.

Lesson 24.6

1. Volume = 175π cu in.
2. Volume = 1125π cu in.
3. Volume = 100 cu in.
4. Volume = 154 cu in.
5. Volume = 108 cu in.
6. Volume = 17 cu in.

Pretest

1. $(4 \times 1{,}000{,}000)$ + $(5 \times 100{,}000)$ + $(8 \times 10{,}000)$ + (7×1000) + (9x 100) + (2×1) + $(4 \times .1)$ + $(5 \times .01)$ + $(3 \times .001)$; Four million five hundred eighty-seven thousand nine hundred two and four hundred and fifty-three thousandths

2. 175 coats
3. 496 miles; 872,960 yards
4. 792
5. 649
6. 2812
7. 1917
8. 83
9. 21
10. 107.118
11. 6.2
12. $7\frac{5}{8}$ kg
13. $7\frac{7}{15}$ L
14. 9
15. −6
16. $x = 27$
17. $x = 5$
18. Distributive Property of Multiplication over Addition
19. Associative Property of Addition
20. 136
21. A(2,3); B(−3,5); C(1,−5); D(−3,−3)
22. $4^3 + 2^2 = 64 + 4 = 68$
23. Area = 120 sq cm; Perimeter = 44 cm
24. Area = 19.625 sq cm; Circumference = 15.75 cm

25. Obtuse; right; acute
26. Scalene; equilateral; isosceles
27. $549.86
28. $3\frac{3}{5}$ or $\frac{18}{5}$
29. 4.625
30. True
31. 1.9, 1.996, 2.009, 2.013, 2.131, 2.202, 2.902, 3.003
32. $130 after 1 year; $135 after two years
33. Mode 38; Median 37.7
34. $3\frac{1}{9}$
35. 33%
36. .2025
37. 1.5667
38. 1
39. Trapezoid; rhombus; square; rectangle; kite;
40. Heptagon; hexagon; pentagon
41. $\frac{71}{13}$
42. $2\frac{11}{16}$
43. $\frac{4}{15}$
44. 15
45. Week 2
46. Apples
47. Kathy
48. 15
49. 94 sq in.
50. Line Segments: $\overline{BD}$, $\overline{DB}$, $\overline{CA}$, $\overline{AC}$, $\overline{HG}$, $\overline{GH}$, $\overline{BE}$, $\overline{AB}$, $\overline{AF}$, $\overline{FA}$; Rays: $\overrightarrow{AC}$, $\overrightarrow{BD}$, $\overrightarrow{BE}$, $\overrightarrow{AF}$, $\overrightarrow{BA}$, $\overrightarrow{AB}$; Line $\overleftrightarrow{AB}$

51.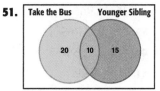

Posttest

1. $(5 \times 1{,}000{,}000)$ + $(1 \times 100{,}000)$ + $(7 \times 10{,}000)$ + (6×1000) + (8×100) + (2×1) + $(4 \times .01)$ + $(5 \times .01)$ + $(3 \times .001)$ + $(9 \times .0001)$; five million one hundred seventy-six thousand eight hundred two and four thousand five hundred thirty-nine ten-thousandths

2. 111 cakes
3. 532 miles
4. 2010
5. 5320
6. 22032
7. 17617
8. 28
9. 21
10. 19.4167
11. 24
12. $15\frac{23}{40}$ kg
13. $21\frac{23}{72}$ L
14. $9\frac{1}{30}$
15. −20
16. $x = 104$
17. $x = 1$
18. Distributive Property of Multiplication over Addition
19. Associative Property of Addition
20. 146
21. A(3,6), B(−5,2), C(2,−4), D(−1,−1)
22. $5^3 + 3^2 = 125 + 9 = 134$
23. Area = 306 sq cm; Perimeter = 70 cm
24. Area = 63.585 sq cm; Circumference = 28.26 cm

Answers

25. Obtuse; right; acute

26. Equilateral; scalene; isosceles

27. $721.05

28. $\frac{38}{5}$; $7\frac{3}{5}$

29. 2.375

30. True

31. .9, 1.004, 1.014, 1.044, 1.141, 1.89, 1.9, 1.996

32. $312.70; $330.40

33. Mode = 36; median = 36

34. $\frac{7}{11}$

35. 46.875%

36. .13125

37. 2350

38. $\frac{1}{4}$

39. Trapezoid; square; rhombus; rectangle; kite

40. Hexagon; pentagon; heptagon

41. $\frac{128}{13}$

42. $5\frac{7}{13}$

43. $\frac{1}{7}$

44. 10 miles

45. Week 2

46. Cauliflower

47. Joe's

48. 15

49. 318 sq in.

50. Line segments: $\overline{YS}$, $\overline{XT}$, $\overline{XR}$, $\overline{YZ}$, $\overline{LM}$, $\overline{ML}$, $\overline{XY}$, $\overline{TX}$, $\overline{RX}$, $\overline{SY}$, $\overline{ZY}$; Rays: $\overrightarrow{XR}$, $\overrightarrow{XT}$, $\overrightarrow{YS}$, $\overrightarrow{YZ}$, $\overrightarrow{XY}$, $\overrightarrow{YX}$; Line $\overleftrightarrow{XY}$

51.
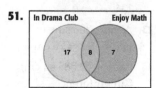

Unit Test Lesson 1-3

1. 311

2. 505

3. 1573

4. 4906

5. 652,576

6. 838

7. 1219

8. 6395

9. 4889

10. 379

11. 21,000; 21,022

12. 55,000; 53,931

13. 67,000; 66,587

14. 71,000; 70,364

15. 90,000; 89,853

16. 200; 193

17. 1400; 1389

18. 28,680,000; 28,716,878

19. 12,000; 11,716

20. 38,000; 37,866

21. 3192

22. 22,356

23. 21,850

24. 30,260

25. 48,766

26. 14

27. 21

28. 58 R4

29. 18 R13

30. 13 R25

31. 72,000; 77,112

32. 300,000; 297,724

33. 24,000,000; 21,996,652

34. 5,600,000; 5,067,270

35. 48,000,000; 46,163,126

36. 3; 3 R11

37. 5; 5 R150

38. 16; 16 R65

39. 120; 121 R65

40. 1000; 1025 R55

41. Hundreds

42. Thousandths

43. Ten millions

44. Hundreths

45. 19415 visitors

46. 559 coins

47. About 120 pages; 123 pages

48. $(1 \times 1000) + (7 \times 100) + (7 \times 10) + (6 \times 1)$

49. Nineteen million, two hundred thirty-eight thousand, nine hundred seventy-six

50. 208,416,000,000 pieces of mail;
$(2 \times 100,000,000,000) + (8 \times 1,000,000,000) + (4 \times 100,000,000) + (1 \times 10,000,000) + (6 \times 1,000,000)$

Unit Test Lessons 4-7

1. $2\frac{3}{7}$

2. $4\frac{5}{6}$

3. 6

4. $10\frac{20}{33}$

5. $\frac{83}{11}$

6. $\frac{69}{13}$

7. $\frac{91}{19}$

8. $\frac{119}{16}$

9. $2\frac{1}{2}$

10. $\frac{6}{49}$

11. $1\frac{8}{11}$

12. $3\frac{8}{39}$

13. $\frac{21}{41}$

14. $\frac{15}{16}$

15. $\frac{9}{31}$

16. $\frac{69}{74}$

17. $1\frac{1}{17}$

18. $5\frac{107}{264}$

19. $\frac{32}{45}$

20. $\frac{33}{175}$

21. $1\frac{82}{99}$

22. $1\frac{11}{133}$

23. $\frac{47}{164}$

24. $3\frac{32}{221}$

25. $\frac{394}{525}$

26. $35\frac{2}{63}$

27. $24\frac{11}{29}$

28. $23\frac{19}{28}$

29. $9\frac{6}{11}$

30. $27\frac{1}{2}$

31. 18

32. $\frac{11}{36}$

33. $1\frac{16}{27}$

34. $4\frac{4}{11}$

35. $\frac{1}{87}$

36. $\frac{3}{47}$

37. $\frac{1}{18}$

38. $\frac{4}{81}$

39. $\frac{5}{83}$

40. $45\frac{1}{2}$

41. 220

42. $1\frac{17}{64}$

43. 1

44. $\frac{9}{16}$

45. No

46. No

47. Yes

48. Yes

49. $x = 15$

50. $x = 62.5$

51. $x = 32$

52. $x = 200$

53. $\dfrac{35}{16}$

54. $\dfrac{5}{9}$

55. 60 miles

56. 24 batches

57. $4\dfrac{5}{16}$ pints

58. 9 times

Unit Test Lessons 8-12

1. 3407.0

2. 334,782.1

3. 65,529.1

4. 12.9

5. 2,467,891.36

6. 12.45

7. 97.01

8. 17.61

9. 467,001.3555

10. 199.1112

11. 1,683,679.5734

12. 8.1943

13. $\dfrac{4}{5}$

14. $\dfrac{7}{8}$

15. $\dfrac{2}{25}$

16. $\dfrac{5}{8}$

17. .6

18. .5333

19. .1875

20. 6.125

21. .819, .6165, .616, .513, .3132, .2126, .122, .1145

22. .5257, .217, .20413, .1243, .05257, .05205, .0487, .0217, .0133

23. 3.472817

24. 6.53518656

25. 6.660933

26. 1.91916

27. 1.428711

28. 2.24946656

29. $6.75

30. $2.78

31. 36.297

32. 2119.175

33. $0.11

34. 7.48935

35. $0.92

36. 2.9768005

37. $6.75

38. 1.478625

39. 6.380989

40. $11.70

41. 23.22

42. 1.419

43. .09; .106575

44. .6362

45. 303.50

46. 13755

47. 90; 90.75

48. 50; 45.61818

49. 320; 308.01465

50. 55; 55.419

51. $\dfrac{21}{50}$

52. 176

53. 12%

54. 28%

55. 127.5%

56. .30315

57. 1.60104

58. .568125

59. $21.51; Yes; $8.49; N/A

60. $51.25

61. $45.28; no

62. $861.35

63. 4%

64. $212.00; $224.00

Unit Test Lessons 13-14

1. Plastic

2. Cigarettes

3. Wood

4. Orlando; Omaha

5. True

6. San Francisco

7. Thursday; Monday

8. Monday

9. $13\dfrac{1}{2}$ hours

10. 2009

11. 2006

12. Chicken

13. Fish

14. Yes. 17% order vegetarian meals

15. Median 9, Mean 17, Range 42

16.

1	9
2	2, 2, 5, 6, 7, 8
3	0, 4, 6, 7
4	4, 4, 4, 5, 8, 8, 9
5	0, 3, 5, 7, 8
6	4, 7

Mode 44, Median 44, Mean 41.3

17. Third quartile range 14; median 22; range of data 45

18. 4

19. 22

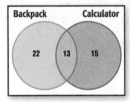

20. 7 people liked both volleyball and football; 47 people in total were surveyed, 20 people liked only volleyball and 20 people liked only football.

21. Yellow marker $\dfrac{7}{20}$; anything but a green marker $\dfrac{15}{20}$ or $\dfrac{3}{4}$

Unit Test Lessons 15-18

1. $8^2 \times 2 + 3^3 = 155$

2. $2^2 \times 4^2 - 3^3 = 37$

3. $5 \times 25 \times 2^2 \times 4^2 + 7^2 - 5^2 = 8024$

4. 1.3654764011×10^7

5. 2.839701×10^4

6. 1.00745×10^{-1}

7. $2.11946680411 \times 10^{10}$

8. 8.13056×10^2

9. 122

10. 84

11. 27

12. 4096

13. 2

14. 10

15. 1

16. Associative Property of Addition

17. Distributive Property of Multiplication over Addition

18. Commutative Property of Addition

19. Identity Property of Multiplication

20. Identity Property of Addition

21. Identity Property of Multiplication

22. Associative Property of Multiplication

23. Zero Property of Addition and Multiplication

24. $x = 7$

25. $x = 37$

26. $x = 14$

27. $x = 30$

28. $x = 5$

29. $x = 6$

30. $x = 7$

31. $x = 14$

32. $x = 13$

33. $x = 54$

Answers

34. $x = 70$

35. $x = 60$

36. D

37. C

38. B

39. A

40. -75

41. -5

42. -9

43. 8

44. (1,3)

45. (4,4)

46. (−5,2)

47. (4,−4)

48. (−4,−2)

49. (7,6)

50. (−2,5)

51. (−6,−6)

52. (−3,8)

53. (3,−8)

54.–59.

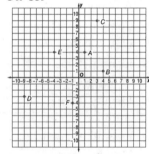

Unit Test Lessons 19-21

1. 1998 inches of trim

2. 136 quart containers

3. The second box weighs the most.

4. 179.75 ft

5. 240 sq ft

6. 24 square ft

7. 35 cu ft

8. 486 miles in a minute; 29,160 miles in an hour; 699,840 miles in a day

9. 8.5 hours; about 3 times

10. 5096 cm

11. 152,750 sq cm

12. 7.913 liters

13. 12 sq cm

14. 362 meters

15. 81.9 cu m

16. 180.34 cm

17. 89.8 quarts; 22.4 gallons

18. 4480 sq ft; 498 sq yd

19. 39.78° C

20. 16,404 ft

21. 35 cu cm

22. 144 cu in.

23. 73.4–78.8° F

24. $2\frac{1}{4}$ hours

Unit Test Lessons 22-24

1. Obtuse

2. Right

3. Acute

4. Acute

5. Obtuse

6. Complementary; angle measures sum to 90°

7. Supplementary; angle measures sum to 180°

8. Complementary; angle measures sum to 90°

9. Neither; angle measures sum to 89°

10. Neither; angle measures sum to 169°

11. Equilateral

12. Scalene

13. Isosceles

14. Scalene

15. Equilateral

16. Scalene

17. Right

18. Acute

19. Acute

20. Acute

21. Obtuse

22. Right

23. Point A

24. $\overline{HG}$, $\overline{BD}$, $\overline{BC}$, $\overline{CD}$

25. $\overline{HG}$

26. $\overline{AG}$, $\overline{AD}$, $\overline{AH}$

27. Cube; square; 6 faces; 12 edges; 8 vertices

28. Rectangular solid; rectangle; 6 faces; 12 edges; 8 vertices

29. Rectangular Pyramid; rectangle; 5; 8; 5

30. Cone; circle; 2 faces; No edges; 1 vertex

31. Triangular Pyramid; Triangle; 4 faces; 6 edges; 4 vertices

32. Triangular Prism; Triangle; 5 faces; 9 edges; 6 vertices

33. Pentagon

34. Hexagon

35. Heptagon

36. Octagon

37. Circumference 18.84; Area 28.26 sq units

38. 148 sq cm

39. 120 wooden blocks